Shorter

Wild Flower Walks

in Dorset

Peter & Margaret Cramb

P. & M. Cramb

First published in 2009
by P. & M. Cramb
32 Pitchers, Salway Ash,
Bridport, Dorset DT6 5QS

Maps based on Ordnance Survey mapping
under Licence No. 100044737

ISBN 978 0 9537746 3 0

British Library Cataloguing-in-Publication Data.
A catalogue record for this book is
available from the British Library.

Printed by Henry Ling Limited,
The Dorset Press, Dorchester DT1 1HD

CONTENTS

Cover photographs
Front: Bluebells on Langdon Hill
Back: Early-purple Orchids

INTRODUCTION

After we published *Wild Flower Walks in Dorset* three years ago, several friends asked if we could come up with some rather less energetic wild flower walks. This book is our response: the ten walks here range from about 2 to 3½ miles and for two of the walks we have given shorter, easier, alternatives.

We hope that these walks will appeal to wild flower lovers of all ages so that parents, children, grandparents, and perhaps even great-grandparents, as well as those with just an hour or two to spare, will be able to enjoy them.

We have aimed to spread the walks across Dorset, although flower-rich areas, such as the coast and the Isle of Purbeck, are better represented than other parts of the county. The walks cover a wide range of different flower habitats with the result that you can see a total of over 300 species on the ten walks.

For each walk we have shown the time of year when the flowers mentioned are usually at their best, although timings vary from season to season depending on weather conditions. You may like to make some adjustment for this, but even if you miss the best times you should still see plenty of flowers. Although the walk details are correct at the time of writing, things inevitably change over a period of time; for example, footpaths are diverted or charges brought in for car parks. You may therefore need to make allowance for such occurrences.

In writing this book we have discovered parts of Dorset new to us and enjoyed finding beautiful wild flowers in some stunning landscapes; we hope that these walks give you as much pleasure as they have given us.

Opposite: *A peaceful summer day at Fiddleford Mill*

ACKNOWLEDGEMENTS

We are most grateful to the following for permission to reproduce copyright material in this book:

H. J. Massingham *English Downland*, Batsford 1936.
> Reproduced with the permission of The Society of Authors as the Literary Representative of the Estate of H. J. Massingham.

Llewelyn Powys *Dorset Essays*, Redcliffe Press Ltd. 1983.
> Reproduced with the permission of Sally Connely.

Andrew Young *The Fly-Orchis* and *Groundsel* from *Complete Poems Andrew Young,* Secker & Warburg 1974.
> Reproduced with the permission of Ruth Lowbury.

We are also grateful to Natural England for permission to use the text of the Countryside Code.

We believe we have obtained all necessary permissions to reproduce copyright material used in this book: should this not be the case we offer our apologies and will ensure that due acknowledgement is made in any reprint.

CARE AND SAFETY

Safety warning

In the interests of safety, please always:

- keep strictly to the route and marked paths.
- observe any indicated diversions.
- be alert when walking along roads.
- take special care in poor weather conditions.

Please also note the specific warnings concerning cliffs in Walks 2 and 7, flooding in Walk 8 and bogs in Walk 9. For all the walks we suggest you use common sense and take appropriate precautions. Always wear stout well-gripping footwear, preferably walking boots, to reduce the risk of slipping.

Bites by ticks can cause Lyme disease; to reduce the risk of bites wear long trousers tucked into socks. If you feel unwell after being bitten, seek medical advice immediately.

Rights of way

All the routes described in the book follow rights of way or permissive paths, or go across access land. Some small lanes and tracks, marked with broken orange lines on the maps, have the status of Unclassified County Roads and carry certain rights for walkers, horse riders, cyclists and motor vehicles.

You may find a compass helpful in following the directions.

Follow The Countryside Code

- Be safe - plan ahead and follow any signs.
- Leave gates and property as you find them.
- Protect plants and animals, and take your litter home.
- Keep dogs under close control.
- Consider other people.

Walk locations ⬤

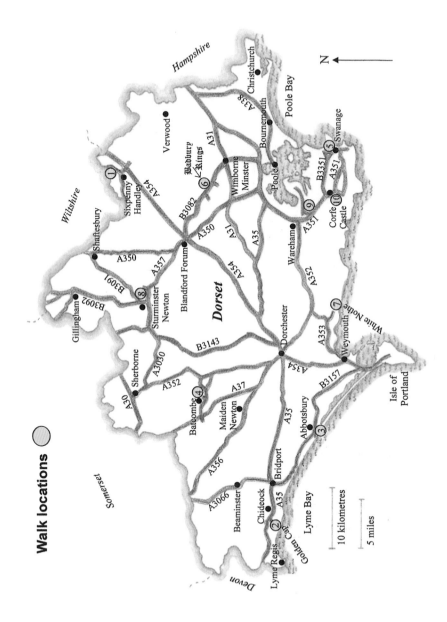

THE WALKS

Pleasures newly found are sweet
When they lie about our feet:

William Wordsworth

WALK 1

SPRING FLOWERS OF ANCIENT WOODLANDS ON THE WILTSHIRE BORDER
Garston and Mistleberry Woods

A spring walk in the far north-east of Dorset. We first walk through the RSPB's Garston Wood nature reserve with its stunning variety of woodland flowers. We then cross farmland to reach a minor road which we follow for a short distance, before joining a footpath taking us up to Mistleberry Wood and another magnificent display of flowers. We continue on the footpath along the Dorset and Wiltshire border, passing close to a partly constructed Iron Age hill-fort, before returning to Garston Wood.

Time of year:	early April to mid-May
Distance:	about 2½ miles (4 km)
Difficulty:	fairly easy, but with one uphill section
Parking:	small RSPB car park off minor road at SU 003 195 (free)
Directions to car park:	from Blandford take the A354 north-east towards Salisbury. Pass through Cashmoor and after 2¾ miles (4½ km) turn left at a roundabout on to the B3081, signposted " Shaftesbury Sixpenny Handley 1 Tollard Royal 5". After 1 mile (1½ km), shortly after entering Sixpenny Handley, turn right, signposted "Deanland 1¼ Bowerchalke 4¼ Newton 1½". After ½ mile (¾ km) bear right at a road junction, signposted "Bowerchalke 4 Ebbesborne Wake 5". Follow the road for a further 1¼ miles (2 km) until you reach the car park on your left.
Ordnance Survey maps:	1:50,000 Landranger 184 Salisbury 1:25,000 Explorer 118 Shaftesbury & Cranborne Chase
Public transport:	none
Refreshments:	in Sixpenny Handley
Toilets:	none

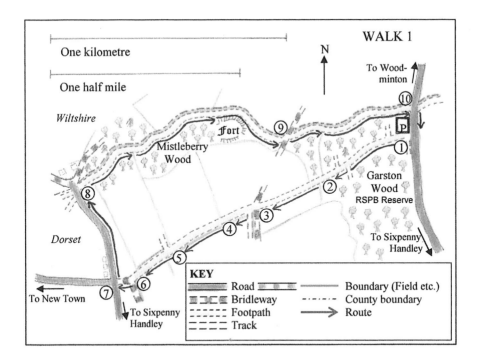

ROUTE

1.   Leave the car park by a kissing gate, next to a large gate, opposite where you drove in. Turn right (roughly west) on to a signposted footpath and continue (roughly west then south-west) through Garston Wood for 500 yards (460 metres), until you reach a kissing gate, waymarked "Sixpenny Handley Round Walk".

   Many woodland flowers grow beside the footpath, including Bluebells, Columbine, Common Twayblade, Early-purple Orchid, Lesser Celandine, Sanicle, Solomon's-seal, Toothwort, Wood Anemone and Wood Spurge.

2.   Go through the kissing gate and continue straight ahead (roughly west) on the footpath, which soon emerges from the wood and crosses a field, for 300 yards (275 metres), until you reach the end of a hedge where the footpath is crossed by a bridleway.

3.   Go straight ahead (roughly west) at the crossing and follow the footpath along the left edge of the field for 175 yards (160 metres) until you reach a gap in the hedge on the far side.

Garston Wood

Garston Wood is part of Cranborne Chase, once a royal hunting forest and now a mixture of woodland and farmland. The wood is one of Dorset's best examples of ancient coppiced woodland and supports a great variety of wild flowers.

As you walk through the wood in early spring surrounded by a spellbinding array of wild flowers it is fascinating to think that little has changed here for many generations - for hundreds of years hazel has been repeatedly cut for timber to produce articles such as hurdles and thatching spars. Coppicing is now carried out by the RSPB in regular cycles to encourage wild flowers, butterflies and other wildlife, while in parts of the wood trees are left to mature to their full size. As a result the wood contains areas at different stages of tree development, helping to increase the number of species present. Garston Wood lies on chalky soil and this also adds to the variety of wild flowers found here.

The age of the wood, its long history of suitable management and favourable soil combine to produce a rich and interesting mixture of wild flowers. You can see here many plants indicating ancient woodland, including Columbine, Sanicle, Solomon's-seal, Toothwort (see page 17), Wood Anemone, Woodruff and Wood Spurge (see page 14).

4. Go through the gap and continue on the footpath (roughly south-west) along the left edge of the next field for 250 yards (230 metres) until you reach a gap in the hedge on the far side.
5. Go through the gap and continue straight ahead (south-west) on the footpath, (waymarked "Sixpenny Handley Round Walk" on a post to your left), along the right edge of the next field for 275 yards (250 metres) until you reach a large metal gate and waymarked stile on the far side.
6. Cross the stile on to a made-up track and continue straight ahead (west) for 50 yards (45 metres) until you reach a road.
7. Turn right on to the road and continue (roughly north then north-west) for 550 yards (500 metres) until it is crossed by a signposted footpath.

Opposite: *A woodland ride in Garston Wood.*

Wood Spurge

"My eyes, wide open, had the run
Of some ten weeds to fix upon;
Among those few, out of the sun,
The woodspurge flowered,
          three cups in one."

From *The Woodspurge*,
D.G. Rossetti

As you walk through Garston Wood, you will often see the distinctive shape of Wood Spurge. Its upright stems are up to 2½ feet (75 cm) tall and surrounded by dark green, oblong, leathery leaves, while at the top are clusters of greenish yellow flower heads.

Each flower head is about 1 inch (2½ cm) across and has no petals or sepals, the petal-like cups containing the flowers being formed of two leaf-like bracts joined together. Within each cup are 4 crescent-shaped glands enclosing several tiny male flowers and a single female flower, together with two further cups of bracts containing flowers. The plants require light and are often found in large patches along woodland rides or in recently coppiced areas, where dormant seeds have burst into life after the shading vegetation has been removed.

Wood Spurge is found across Dorset, usually in old woodlands or on hedge banks; it also sometimes grows on undercliffs, particularly on Portland. The plant is an indicator of ancient woodland.

Opposite left*: Bugle*

Opposite right*: Butcher's-broom or Knee-holly - the spiny "leaves" are actually flattened stems.*

8. Turn right (roughly north-east) on to the footpath (waymarked "Sixpenny Handley Round Walk"), ignoring a bridleway a little further on. Follow the footpath, at first uphill, along the right edge of woods, then through them and, finally, along their left edge (generally north-east then east), for ¾ mile (1¼ km) until the footpath is crossed by a bridleway. Shortly before the crossing you will pass a partly constructed Iron Age hill-fort in the woods on your right.

    There are magical glades of Bluebells along here, and other woodland plants such as Butcher's-broom, Early-purple Orchid, Goldilocks Buttercup, Ramsons, Sanicle, Townhall Clock, the attractive Wood Melick grass, Woodruff and Wood-sorrel.

9. Turn left, then quickly right, at the crossing, staying on the waymarked footpath, and continue (roughly east) along the left edge of woods for 650 yards (600 metres) until you reach a road.

    The footpath is bordered by great drifts of Wood Melick, while clumps of Toothwort grow at the foot of hazel.

10. Turn right (south) on to the road and continue for 100 yards (90 metres) until you reach the car park on your right.

Toothwort

You will see Toothwort quite frequently in Garston Wood, growing in clumps around the base of hazel trees. The plant is parasitic on their roots, attaching itself with small suckers and diverting their sap.

The white or pale pink downy stems grow to around 8 inches (20 cm) tall and, instead of leaves, carry whitish scales. The off-white or pink two-lipped flowers all grow on one side of the stem and are about ¾ inch (2 cm) long. They look like a row of stained teeth, giving the plant its name. Toothwort has a strange, almost ghostly, appearance and its country name of Corpse Flower came from the belief that it grows where bodies are buried.

In Dorset, Toothwort grows in old woods, usually on chalky soils. It is commonest in Cranborne Chase and other parts of the north-east of the county, but is also found in the west. As with Wood Spurge, it is an indicator of ancient woodland.

Opposite*: Toothwort*

Below left*: Bluebell*
Below right*: A magical glade of bluebells in Mistleberry Wood.*

"And like a skylit water stood
The bluebells in the azured wood."
From *A Shropshire Lad*
A.E. Housman

Some of the flowers you may see on this walk

Barren Strawberry *(Potentilla sterilis)*
Black Bryony *(Tamus communis)*
Bluebell *(Hyacinthoides non-scripta)*
Bugle *(Ajuga reptans)*
Bush Vetch *(Vicia sepium)*
Butcher's-broom *(Ruscus aculeatus)*
Columbine *(Aquilegia vulgaris)*
Common Dog-violet *(Viola riviniana)*
Common Field-speedwell *(Veronica persica)*
Common Twayblade *(Listera ovata)*
Cow Parsley, Queen Anne's Lace *(Anthriscus sylvestris)*
Dandelions *(Taraxacum agg.)*
Dog's Mercury *(Mercurialis perennis)*
Early Dog-violet *(Viola reichenbachiana)*
Early-purple Orchid *(Orchis mascula)*
Field Madder *(Sherardia arvensis)*
Garlic Mustard *(Alliaria petiolata)*
Germander Speedwell *(Veronica chamaedrys)*
Goldilocks Buttercup *(Ranunculus auricomus)*
Greater Stitchwort *(Stellaria holostea)*
Ground-ivy *(Glechoma hederacea)*
Herb-Robert *(Geranium robertianum)*

Ivy-leaved Speedwell *(Veronica hederifolia)*
Keeled-fruited Cornsalad *(Valerianella carinata)*
Lesser Celandine *(Ranunculus ficaria)*
Lords-and-Ladies, Cuckoo-pint *(Arum maculatum)*
Pignut *(Conopodium majus)*
Primrose *(Primula vulgaris)*
Ramsons *(Allium ursinum)*
Red Dead-nettle *(Lamium purpureum)*
Sanicle *(Sanicula europaea)*
Solomon's-seal *(Polygonatum multiflorum)*
Toothwort *(Lathraea squamaria)*
Townhall Clock, Moschatel *(Adoxa moschatellina)*
White Dead-nettle *(Lamium album)*
Wood Anemone *(Anemone nemorosa)*
Woodruff *(Galium odoratum)*
Wood-sorrel *(Oxalis acetosella)*
Wood Speedwell *(Veronica montana)*
Wood Spurge *(Euphorbia amygdaloides)*
Yellow Archangel *(Lamiastrum galeobdolon)*

Opposite: In early spring parts of Garston Wood are carpeted with Lesser Celandines and Wood Anemones.

WALK 2

BLUEBELLS AND BROOMRAPES ON THE
WEST DORSET COAST
Langdon Hill and Golden Cap

A spring walk in the south-west of Dorset. Starting in Langdon Hill Wood, we see magnificent displays of Bluebells in late April and early May as we skirt its western edge. We then cross fields to the summit of Golden Cap, with its own special flowers and panoramic views.

After partly retracing our steps, we cross more fields to reach a minor road with hedge banks rich in spring flowers. We follow this and another road to return to our starting point.

Please keep well away from the cliff edges while you are on the summit of Golden Cap.

Time of year:	early April to mid-May
Distance:	about 2¾ miles (4½ km)
	short route: about 1½ miles (2½ km)
Difficulty:	mostly easy but with two steep sections
	short route: easy
Parking:	National Trust car park off minor road at SY 412 930
	(charge, but free to National Trust members)
Directions to car park:	from Bridport take the A35 westwards. After passing through Chideock take the first turn on the left. After 75 yards (70 metres) turn left again (signposted "Golden Cap Car Park"). Follow the road for 400 yards (360 metres) until you reach the car park on your right.
Ordnance Survey maps:	1:50,000 Landranger 193 Taunton & Lyme Regis
	1:25,000 Explorer 116 Lyme Regis & Bridport
Public transport:	31 bus between Weymouth and Axminster and X53 bus between Poole and Exeter stop in Chideock (check timetables)
Refreshments:	in Chideock and Seatown
Toilets:	none

20

ROUTE

1. Leave the car park by the gate at the far right end from where you drove in. Follow the forest track (roughly north, then north-west and west) for 450 yards (410 metres) until a footpath branches off to the right just before a wooden bench.

   There are seas of Bluebells in the woods on both sides of the track in late April and early May.

2. Turn right on to the footpath (roughly west) and follow it along the edge of Langdon Hill Wood (generally south) for ¾ mile (1¼ km) until you reach a junction with another footpath at a signpost. There are attractive views ahead (roughly south) to Golden Cap and to your right (roughly west) over the sea to Lyme Regis and the East Devon coast.

   You will see many wild flowers along the woodland edge, including Common Dog-violet, Greater Stitchwort, Ramsons, Wood Speedwell and Yellow Archangel, while the wood to your left is carpeted with a stunning display of Bluebells in late April and early May.

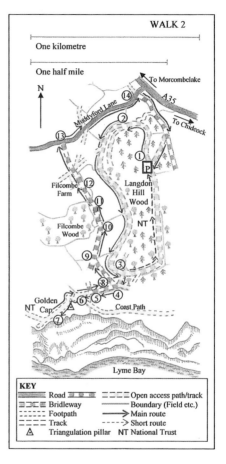

3. Turn right (south) at the junction on to the other footpath (signposted "To Coast Path Golden Cap") and follow it downhill (south) for 50 yards (45 metres) until you reach a kissing gate.

4. Go through the kissing gate, turn right (west) and go through a small gate waymarked for two bridleways, next to a large gate, into a field. Take the bridleway running along the left edge (roughly west) towards the summit of Golden Cap. Continue for 200 yards (180 metres) until you reach a double stile and gate at the far end.

   Three-nerved Sandwort is sometimes found beneath this stile.

Golden Cap

At 626 feet (191 metres), Golden Cap is the highest cliff on the south coast of England and a prominent landmark, visible from miles around.

Its name comes from its top of golden yellow sandstone which lies above Jurassic clays. As with much of the surrounding coastline, it is slowly eroding and frequent landslips form undercliffs where uncommon plants such as Marsh Helleborine and Slender Centaury are found.

> "Golden Cap was receding, foot by foot, century after century, yet the process of destruction was slow. Though the yellow edge of cliff touched the flat top and the area of the summit had aforetime been much more extensive, a great many acres still remained to fight dauntlessly an ultimately losing battle."
>
> From *The Treasure of Golden Cap*,
> Bennet Copplestone

From the triangulation pillar at the eastern end of the summit you have magnificent views east (on your left when facing the sea) to Thorncombe Beacon, West Bay, Burton Cliff, Abbotsbury (see Walk 3), Chesil Bank and Portland. From the western end of the summit you have equally splendid views west to Stonebarrow Hill, Charmouth, Lyme Regis and the East Devon coast, with, just beneath you, the remains of St. Gabriel's Church.

Despite its exposed position, Golden Cap is a special place for wild flowers. Growing on the acid soil of the summit is an area of heathland vegetation with Bell Heather, Gorse, Greater Broomrape (see page 26), Heather, Heath Milkwort and Tormentil. Found close to the cliff edge are Bird's-foot, Broom, Buck's-horn Plantain, Common Stork's-bill and Mouse-ear-hawkweed, and, reflecting the influence of the sea, Sea Campion, Sea Mouse-ear and Thrift.

If your visit is on a fine late spring day you may also see the tiny Green Hairstreak butterfly flying close to its foodplant, Gorse.

Opposite: *View from Golden Cap to the east with a rock garden of Sea Campion and Thrift in the foreground.*

5. Cross one of the stiles into the next field and take the footpath straight across (roughly west) signposted "To Coast Path Golden Cap". Continue for 75 yards (70 metres) uphill until you reach a kissing gate on the far side.

6. Go through the kissing gate on to the coast path, signposted "Coast Path Golden Cap" and follow the winding stepped path up the hill for 150 yards (135 metres) until you reach the triangulation pillar at the summit (see 'Golden Cap' page 23).

7. After you have looked round the summit retrace your steps to the small gate you went through early in stage 4.

8. Do not go through the gate but take the bridleway going uphill to your left (roughly north-west). [NB. The line of this bridleway, which runs slightly to the left of the edge of Langdon Hill Wood, is, at first, very faint: do not take the more obvious route further left (roughly west) leading to a large gate]. Continue (roughly north-west) along the bridleway for 200 yards (180 metres) until the ground falls and you reach a stile and gate.

9. Cross the stile into the next field and continue on the bridleway (roughly north) downhill for 225 yards (210 metres) until you reach another stile and gate. As you cross the field there are good views of Chardown Hill, Lambert's Castle (in the distance) and Hardown Hill to your left and Langdon Hill to your right.

10. Cross the stile into the next field and continue on the bridleway (roughly north) for 150 yards (135 metres) until you reach a stile and gate on your left.
    There is a large yellowish area of Opposite-leaved Golden-saxifrage on the edge of Filcombe Wood to your left.

11. Cross the stile and continue on the bridleway (roughly north) for 100 yards (90 metres) until you reach a gate close to farm buildings. From here you have another excellent view left (roughly west) over the sea to Lyme Regis and the East Devon coast.

12. Go through the gate and continue (roughly north) on the bridleway, which soon becomes a made-up track, for 350 yards (320 metres), passing Filcombe Farm on your left and then following a signpost to "Morcombelake", until you reach a road.

13. Turn right (roughly east) on to the road and follow it uphill (roughly east then north-east) for 550 yards (500 metres) until you reach a junction with another road on your right.
    The hedgebanks along the road are rich in spring flowers, including Alexanders, Bluebells, Cuckooflower, Greater Stitchwort, Lesser Celandine, Ramsons, Townhall Clock and Yellow Archangel. There are also attractive ferns such as Black Spleenwort, Hart's-tongue and Polypody.

Above: Looking west from Golden Cap to Charmouth, Lyme Regis and the East Devon coast.

Right: Ramsons

14. Turn right (roughly south-east) at the junction (signposted "Golden Cap Car Park") and follow the road (roughly south-east) for 400 yards (360 metres) until you reach the entrance to the car park on your right.

Greater Broomrape

Usually visible from early May, Greater Broomrape is found around the summit of Golden Cap, growing close to Gorse bushes. It is parasitic on their roots and closely related to Toothwort (see page 17).

The brownish flowers grow in impressive tall spikes; these can reach 3 feet (90 cm) in favourable conditions, although on the windswept summit of Golden Cap they are rarely half of this height. Each flower is about 1 inch (2½ cm) long and has two lips, the lower with three lobes. Long pointed brown bracts trail beneath, giving the spikes an exotic appearance. As with Toothwort, there are no leaves and in their place pointed brown scales grow on the lower stems.

Greater Broomrape is very rare in Dorset with only one other site currently known, although it was formerly found in about twenty others. The reasons for its decline in Dorset, and a similar trend in Britain as a whole, are not known.

SHORT ROUTE

(a)   Follow the main route to the end of stage 2.

(b)   Go straight ahead (east) at the junction on to the other footpath and follow it uphill for a few yards until it meets a forest track.

(c)   Turn right (east) on to the forest track and follow it (east then north-east and north) for ½ mile (800 metres) until you reach the car park. There are good views to your right (roughly east) of Chideock and, further round to the right (roughly south-east), of Thorncombe Beacon, the sea and, in the distance, Portland.

You will see beautiful drifts of Bluebells in the woods to the left of the track in late April and early May.

Some of the flowers you may see on this walk

Alexanders *(Smyrnium olusatrum)*
Barren Strawberry *(Potentilla sterilis)*
Bird's-foot *(Ornithopus perpusillus)*
Black Bryony *(Tamus communis)*
Bluebell *(Hyacinthoides non-scripta)*
Broom *(Cytisus scoparius)*
Buck's-horn Plantain *(Plantago coronopus)*
Bugle *(Ajuga reptans)*
Bulbous Buttercup *(Ranunculus bulbosus)*
Bush Vetch *(Vicia sepium)*
Cat's-ear *(Hypochaeris radicata)*
Climbing Corydalis *(Ceratocapnos claviculata)*
Common Chickweed *(Stellaria media)*
Common Dog-violet *(Viola riviniana)*
Common Mouse-ear *(Cerastium fontanum)*
Common Stork's-bill *(Erodium cicutarium)*
Cow Parsley, Queen Anne's Lace *(Anthriscus sylvestris)*
Creeping Buttercup *(Ranunculus repens)*
Cuckooflower *(Cardamine pratensis)*
Daisy *(Bellis perennis)*
Dandelions *(Taraxacum agg.)*
Dog's Mercury *(Mercurialis perennis)*
Garlic Mustard *(Alliaria petiolata)*
Germander Speedwell *(Veronica chamaedrys)*
Gorse *(Ulex europaeus)*
Greater Broomrape *(Orobanche rapum-genistae)*
Greater Stitchwort *(Stellaria holostea)*
Ground-ivy *(Glechoma hederacea)*
Heath Milkwort *(Polygala serpyllifolia)*
Herb-Robert *(Geranium robertianum)*

Hogweed *(Heracleum sphondylium)*
Ivy-leaved Speedwell *(Veronica hederifolia)*
Ivy-leaved Toadflax *(Cymbalaria muralis)*
Lesser Celandine *(Ranunculus ficaria)*
Lesser Trefoil *(Trifolium dubium)*
Lords-and-Ladies, Cuckoo-pint *(Arum maculatum)*
Meadow Buttercup *(Ranunculus acris)*
Mouse-ear-hawkweed *(Pilosella officinarum)*
Opposite-leaved Golden-saxifrage *(Chrysosplenium oppositifolium)*
Primrose *(Primula vulgaris)*
Ramsons *(Allium ursinum)*
Red Campion *(Silene dioica)*
Red Clover *(Trifolium pratense)*
Red Dead-nettle *(Lamium purpureum)*
Ribwort Plantain *(Plantago lanceolata)*
Sea Campion *(Silene uniflora)*
Sea Mouse-ear *(Cerastium diffusum)*
Sheep's Sorrel *(Rumex acetosella)*
Three-nerved Sandwort *(Moehringia trinervia)*
Thrift, Sea Pink *(Armeria maritima)*
Tormentil *(Potentilla erecta)*
Townhall Clock, Moschatel *(Adoxa moschatellina)*
Wavy Bitter-cress *(Cardamine flexuosa)*
Wild Strawberry *(Fragaria vesca)*
Wood Avens, Herb Bennet *(Geum urbanum)*
Wood-sorrel *(Oxalis acetosella)*
Wood Speedwell *(Veronica montana)*
Yellow Archangel *(Lamiastrum galeobdolon)*

WALK 3

SPRING FLOWERS AT ABBOTSBURY
Chapel Hill and the Chesil Bank

A late spring walk on the West Dorset coast. We start by following the coast path south-east along the back of the Chesil Bank. Continuing on the path, we climb the lower slopes of Chapel Hill with outstanding views over Abbotsbury Swannery, the Fleet and the Chesil Bank to Portland.

Leaving the coast path, we skirt the east side of the hill with good views of Abbotsbury's historic buildings. We then follow tracks round the north and west sides before rejoining the coast path and retracing our steps to the car park.

Time of year:	early May to early June
Distance:	about 2¾ miles (4½ km)
Difficulty:	fairly easy, but with one uphill section
Parking:	Abbotsbury Beach car park off minor road at SY 560 846 (charge)
Directions to car park:	from Weymouth take the B3157 west towards Bridport. After passing through Abbotsbury, take the first turn on the left (signposted "Sub-Tropical Gardens ¼ Chesil Beach ¾"). Follow the road for ¾ mile (1¼ km), passing Abbotsbury Gardens on your left, until you reach the car park on your left shortly before the beach.
Ordnance Survey maps:	1:50,000 Landranger 194 Dorchester & Weymouth 1:25,000 Explorer OL 15 Purbeck & South Dorset
Public transport:	X53 bus between Poole and Exeter stops in Abbotsbury village (check timetable)
Refreshments:	at car park (peak times), Abbotsbury Gardens (free entry to restaurant) and in Abbotsbury village
Toilets:	at car park

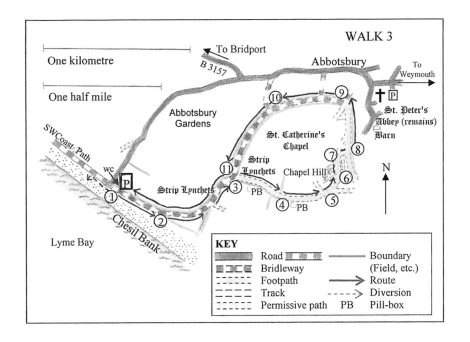

ROUTE

1. Leave the car park by the exit to the beach and turn left (roughly south-east) on to the coast path, which you will be following until stage 8. Follow the path along the back of the shingle beach (roughly south-east then east) for 350 yards (320 metres) until you reach a stone marked "Abbotsbury 1 Swannery 1¾".

   On your left is a hedge of Tamarisk, while Bird's-foot Clover, Eastern Gladiolus, Hound's-tongue, Rosy Garlic and Sea Campion grow at the back of the beach.

2. Bear left (roughly east) at the marker stone and, leaving the shingle beach, continue on the coast path (east then north-east) for 700 yards (640 metres) until you reach a stile on your right signposted "Swannery ¾" (ignoring an earlier stile on your right waymarked "Countryside Commission").You will have a good view of St. Catherine's Chapel from the path.

   Beside the path is a colourful display of flowers including Comfreys (with blue, mauve, pink or white flowers), Hemlock Water-dropwort, Red Campion, Stinking Iris, Water Figwort and Yellow Iris.

29

3. Cross the stile into a field and continue on the coast path (roughly east then south-east) up Chapel Hill for 400 yards (360 metres), passing a wartime pill-box on your right, until you reach a gate to the right of a wall. On the hill behind you will see strip lynchets (long narrow terraces resulting from medieval agriculture), while to your right is a magnificent view over Abbotsbury Swannery, the Fleet and the Chesil Bank to Portland.

4. Go through the gate into an area of rough grassland and continue (roughly east) on the coast path for 250 yards (230 metres), passing another pill-box on your right, until you reach a stone marked "Abbotsbury ½ Chapel ¼ Swannery ¼".

   Henbane grows on the hill to the left of the path.

5. Bear left (roughly north) at the marker stone, following the direction to Abbotsbury, and continue for 100 yards (90 metres) until you reach a stile at the edge of a wood.

6. Cross the stile and continue (north) on the coast path through the wood for 150 yards (135 metres) until you reach a gate and stile at the far end. Cross the stile into a field and continue (north) on the path for 150 yards (135 metres) until you come to a fork at a waymarked post. From here you have an excellent view to your right of Abbotsbury Church and the Abbey Barn.

7. Take the right hand fork (roughly north-east), staying on the coast path, and continue for 25 yards (23 metres) until you meet a footpath running along the side of a wall.

8. Turn left (north) on to this footpath (signposted "Abbotsbury St. Catherine's Chapel"), leaving the coast path. Continue on the footpath (north) for 325 yards (300 metres) until you reach a large metal gate with a kissing gate to its left. [N.B. Some minor changes to the arrangement of gates in this stage have been proposed, but not put into effect at the time of writing].

   Ivy-leaved Toadflax, Pellitory-of-the-wall and Wall Pennywort grow on the wall.

9. Go through the kissing gate, turn left (west) on to a track (signposted "Chesil Beach 1") and continue (roughly west) for 700 yards (640 metres) until you reach a large gate at a junction with another track.

10. Go through the gate and turn left (roughly south-west) on to the track (signposted "Chesil Beach ¾") and follow it (roughly south-west then south) for 600 yards (550 metres) until you reach the stile, on your left, where you took the coast path up Chapel Hill at stage 3.

11. Retrace your steps to the car park.

Opposite*: Abbotsbury Church from the east side of Chapel Hill.*

Henbane

"On hills of dust the henbane's faded green,
And pencil'd flower of sickly scent is seen;"

From *The Borough*,
George Crabbe

Henbane is found scattered around the southern slopes of Chapel Hill, usually in ground disturbed by burrowing animals.

The plants are about 2½ feet (75 cm) tall with crowded spikes of pale yellow trumpet-shaped flowers flanked by leaves. Each flower is about 1¼ inches (3 cm) across with a dark purple centre and attractive purple veins, while the leaves are jagged-edged and very hairy. The plants have a strong unpleasant smell and all parts are highly poisonous. They were the source of the poison Dr. Crippen used to murder his wife in 1910 but, more productively, extracts have been used medicinally since ancient times as a pain killer and sedative.

Henbane is biennial and sometimes appears to vanish the year after flowering, only to reappear again the following year. It is scarce in Dorset and usually confined to cliffs, beaches and other places close to the sea. It has declined in recent years, both here and in Britain as a whole, probably due to the increased use of herbicides.

Opposite: Henbane
Below: Henbane on Chapel Hill, Abbotsbury

Sea Pea

To find Sea Pea, leave the car park by the exit to the beach and turn right (roughly north-west). Walk for 200 yards (180 metres) along the road running parallel to the beach until you reach the end of a line of bushes on your left. Turn left and climb to the top of the shingle bank where you will see several large patches of Sea Pea (see diversion on the map).

The plants are only a few inches tall, but can form patches 10 feet (3 metres) or more across. The flowers are about ¾ inch (2 cm) long with purple wings, fading to blue, and whitish centres; they grow in long-stalked heads and have a pleasant, unusual smell. The leaves each have 4-5 pairs of bluish green, attractively veined, slightly fleshy leaflets, usually with a tendril at the end.

As with other plants growing in the exposed conditions of the Chesil Bank, Sea Pea is specially adapted to survive the drying effects of high wind and salt spray. Its roots grow deep into the shingle to extract as much fresh water as possible, while its low height and fleshy leaves help to reduce water loss.

In Dorset, Sea Pea is confined to the shingle of the Chesil Bank where it is abundant in places; in Britain as a whole it is scarce. Besides Dorset, one of its strongholds is the Suffolk coast, where it is said that the plants once kept local people alive during a famine.

Opposite above: *Rosy Garlic*
Below: *Stinking Iris*

Some of the flowers you may see on this walk

Alexanders *(Smyrnium olusatrum)*
Babington's Leek *(Allium ampeloprasum* var. *babingtonii)*
Bird's-foot Clover *(Trifolium ornithopodioides)*
Bittersweet, Woody Nightshade *(Solanum dulcamara)*
Black Bryony *(Tamus communis)*
Bluebell *(Hyacinthoides non-scripta)*
Bristly Oxtongue *(Picris echioides)*
Buck's-horn Plantain *(Plantago coronopus)*
Bush Vetch *(Vicia sepium)*
Cat's-ear *(Hypochaeris radicata)*
Cleavers, Sticky Willy *(Galium aparine)*
Comfreys *(Symphytum agg.)*
Common Bird's-foot-trefoil, Eggs-and-Bacon *(Lotus corniculatus)*
Common Chickweed *(Stellaria media)*
Common Field-speedwell *(Veronica persica)*
Common Knapweed, Hardheads *(Centaurea nigra)*
Common Sorrel *(Rumex acetosa)*
Common Mallow *(Malva sylvestris)*
Common Mouse-ear *(Cerastium fontanum)*
Common Toadflax *(Linaria vulgaris)*
Common Vetch *(Vicia sativa)*
Cow Parsley, Queen Anne's Lace *(Anthriscus sylvestris)*
Creeping Buttercup *(Ranunculus repens)*
Creeping Cinquefoil *(Potentilla reptans)*
Curled Dock *(Rumex crispus)*
Cut-leaved Crane's-bill *(Geranium dissectum)*

Dewberry *(Rubus caesius)*
Dove's-foot Crane's-bill *(Geranium molle)*
Eastern Gladiolus *(Gladiolus communis)*
Field Bindweed *(Convolvulus arvensis)*
Field Forget-me-not *(Myosotis arvensis)*
Garlic Mustard *(Alliaria petiolata)*
Germander Speedwell *(Veronica chamaedrys)*
Goat's-beard *(Tragopogon pratensis* ssp. *minor)*
Greater Knapweed *(Centaurea scabiosa)*
Greater Plantain *(Plantago major)*
Hedge Bindweed *(Calystegia sepium)*
Hedge Woundwort *(Stachys sylvatica)*
Hemlock Water-dropwort *(Oenanthe crocata)*
Henbane *(Hyoscyamus niger)*
Herb-Robert *(Geranium robertianum)*
Hogweed *(Heracleum sphondylium)*
Hound's-tongue *(Cynoglossum officinale)*
Ivy-leaved Toadflax *(Cymbalaria muralis)*
Lesser Trefoil *(Trifolium dubium)*
Lords-and-Ladies, Cuckoo-pint *(Arum maculatum)*
Meadow Buttercup *(Ranunculus acris)*
Meadow Vetchling *(Lathyrus pratensis)*
Mouse-ear-hawkweed *(Pilosella officinarum)*
Musk Thistle, Nodding Thistle *(Carduus nutans)*
Nipplewort *(Lapsana communis)*

Oxeye Daisy *(Leucanthemum vulgare)*
Pellitory-of-the-wall *(Parietaria judaica)*
Pink-sorrel *(Oxalis articulata)*
Prickly Sow-thistle *(Sonchus asper)*
Red Campion *(Silene dioica)*
Red Clover *(Trifolium pratense)*
Red Valerian *(Centranthus ruber)*
Ribwort Plantain *(Plantago lanceolata)*
Rosy Garlic *(Allium roseum)*
Sea Beet *(Beta vulgaris* ssp. *maritima)*
Sea Campion *(Silene uniflora)*
Sea Mouse-ear *(Cerastium diffusum)*
Sea Pea *(Lathyrus japonicus)*
Silverweed *(Potentilla anserina)*
Slender Thistle *(Carduus tenuiflorus)*
Smooth Sow-thistle *(Sonchus oleraceus)*
Spotted Medick *(Medicago arabica)*
Stinking Iris, Gladdon *(Iris foetidissima)*
Thrift, Sea Pink *(Armeria maritima)*
Wall Pennywort, Navelwort *(Umbilicus rupestris)*
Water-cress *(Rorippa nasturtium-aquaticum)*
Water Figwort *(Scrophularia auriculata)*
White Campion *(Silene latifolia)*
White Clover *(Trifolium repens)*
White Dead-nettle *(Lamium album)*
Wild Clary *(Salvia verbenaca)*
Wild Parsnip *(Pastinaca sativa* var. *sativa)*
Wood Avens, Herb Bennet *(Geum urbanum)*
Yellow Iris *(Iris pseudacorus)*

Opposite*: Stems of Garlic Mustard standing upright behind the delicate flowers and fern-like leaves of Herb-Robert.*

WALK 4

DOWNLAND AND WOODLAND FLOWERS
IN THE HEART OF DORSET
Batcombe Down ----- and up again!

A late spring walk on chalk downland and along woodland edges in central
Dorset. Starting at the top of Hilfield Hill we follow a minor road for a short
distance before crossing farmland to reach Batcombe Down. Here we have
glorious views to the north and see a variety of spring flowers of chalk downland.

We then descend over the Down to join a minor road close to the village of
Batcombe, before following this road uphill between verges abundant with
woodland flowers. After a steep final section, we reach the top of Hilfield Hill and
return to our starting point.

Time of year:	early May to late June (woodland best in May, downland in June)
Distance:	about 2¼ miles (3½ km)
Difficulty:	fairly strenuous with steep hills
Parking:	Dorset County Council Hilfield Hill Picnic Site car park at ST 637 040 (free) [very narrow entrance: maximum width 2.2 metres]
Directions to car park:	from Dorchester take the A37 northwards. Pass through Grimstone and after nearly 7 miles (11 km) [ignoring an earlier right turn signposted "Batcombe 1¼ Minterne Magna 4"] turn right on to a minor road (signposted "Batcombe 2¼ Minterne Magna 5") almost opposite a left turn (signposted "Holywell Evershot 1½"). Continue on this road for 3 miles (5 km) until, shortly after passing a left turn (signposted "To the Friary ½ Hilfield 1 Batcombe 1½"), you reach the car park on your left.
Ordnance Survey maps:	1:50,000 Landranger 194 Dorchester & Weymouth 1:25,000 Explorer 117 Cerne Abbas & Bere Regis
Public transport:	none
Refreshments:	in Cerne Abbas and Evershot
Toilets:	none

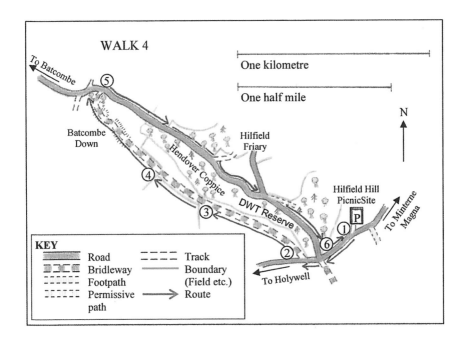

WALK 4

One kilometre

One half mile

N

To Batcombe

⑤

Batcombe
Down

Hendover Coppice

Hilfield
Friary

④

③

DWT Reserve

Hilfield Hill
PicnicSite

P

To Minterne Magna

②

⑥

①

To Holywell

KEY

▬▬▬	Road	= = = =	Track
▰▰▰	Bridleway	———	Boundary
- - - -	Footpath		(Field etc.)
- - - -	Permissive path	——▶	Route

ROUTE

1. Leave the car park by the exit to the road and turn right. Follow the road (roughly south-west) for 300 yards (275 metres), passing a road junction on your right, until, shortly beyond the entrance to Dorset Wildlife Trust's Hendover Coppice nature reserve, you reach a gate with a sign for a bridleway on your right.

2. Go through the gate into a field and follow the bridleway (roughly north-west) across the right side of the field for 750 yards (685 metres) until you reach a waymarked gate in the far right hand corner, slightly to the right of an unwaymarked gate.
    As you cross the field you will see carpets of Bluebells in Hendover Coppice over the fence to your right in early May.

3. Go through the waymarked gate into the next field and continue on the bridleway (roughly north-west) along its left edge for 300 yards (275 metres) until you reach a waymarked gate ahead of you. From this field you have superb views over the Blackmore Vale with Yeovil slightly to your right (roughly north).

False Oxlip

As you pass through the scrubby wood below Batcombe Down, you may come across a plant which seems to be part Primrose and part Cowslip. This is not an illusion, for the plant is their hybrid, False Oxlip.

As the three drawings below show, the features of False Oxlip (centre) are roughly midway between those of its parents. The flowers are yellow, about ¾ inch (2 cm) across and grow in small clusters; Primrose (left) has pale yellow, larger flowers growing alone, while Cowslip's (right) are deep yellow, smaller and grow in larger clusters. Similarly, the leaves of False Oxlip narrow to the base, while those of Primrose taper more gradually and Cowslip's narrow abruptly.

Just as it combines the features of its parents, False Oxlip occupies habitats where they overlap: while Primrose is typically found in woodland and Cowslip in grassland, their offspring inhabits woodland edges and scrub.

False Oxlip is found scattered throughout much of Dorset, but is usually only seen in small numbers: it is worth looking for wherever the two parents are both present. Despite similarities in appearance, it is quite separate from the true Oxlip, which in Britain grows mostly in East Anglia.

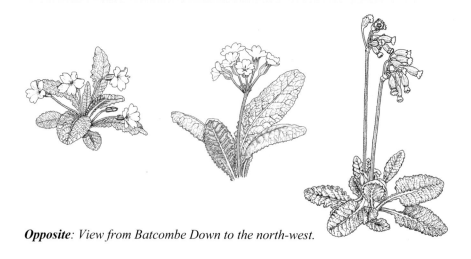

Opposite: *View from Batcombe Down to the north-west.*

Fly Orchid

"Not of the earth or of this earth's sky,
   Nor of any rash and common hour
Is this brown-winged immortal fly,
   This flower-like fly upon a flower."

From *The Fly-Orchis*,
Andrew Young

As Andrew Young suggests, the flower of this unusual-looking orchid can easily be mistaken for a resting insect. So successful is this disguise that the flowers are pollinated by small male wasps which mistake them for females and attempt to mate with them.

Found beside the road you follow in stage 5, the plants are usually about 12-18 inches (30-45 cm) tall with a thin spike of well-spaced flowers at the top of the stem. Each flower is around ½ inch (1¼ cm) across, with a velvety chocolate brown lip - the body and folded wings of the insect - beneath two very narrow petals of similar colour - its antennae - and three green sepals behind.

The shiny leaves are narrow and pointed, growing mostly near the base of the stem. Both stems and leaves are a pale green, which merges into the background vegetation, making the plants difficult to find, even if you know where they are!

Fly Orchid is found in Dorset within and around deciduous woodland on chalky soils. It has declined sharply over the past century and is currently known from only five sites, compared with a previous total of nearly thirty. The reasons for this steep decline are not known. It has also declined in Britain as a whole over the same period and is now regarded as being vulnerable to extinction in the wild.

Opposite*: View towards Telegraph Hill from the road.*

4. Go through the gate and continue on the bridleway (roughly north-west) across Batcombe Down, first close to a fence on your right, then downhill between chalky banks, with the village of Batcombe ahead of you below. *There are many chalk-loving flowers on the Down, including Common Rock-rose, Common Spotted-orchid, Crosswort, Fairy Flax, Horseshoe Vetch, Salad Burnet, Squinancywort and Wild Thyme.*
After 350 yards (320 metres) the bridleway swings briefly to the left (roughly west) before turning right (roughly north). Continue to follow it for a further 200 yards (180 metres), passing through a scrubby wood, until you reach a metal gate at a road.
False Oxlip grows in the wood.

5. Turn right on to the road and follow it (generally south-east) for 1 mile (about 1½ km), passing a road junction on your left, until you reach a T-junction at the top of the hill. As you walk along the road you have an excellent view to your half left (roughly east) towards Telegraph Hill.
The verges beside the road are rich in woodland flowers such as Common Twayblade, Dog's Mercury, Early-purple Orchid, Fly Orchid, Ramsons, Red Campion, Sanicle and Woodruff. The attractive Wood Melick grass also thrives here, while Herb-Paris grows on the edge of Hendover Coppice to your right.

6. Turn left at the junction and follow the road (roughly north-east) for 220 yards (200 metres) until you reach the car park on your left.

Some of the flowers you may see on this walk

Agrimony *(Agrimonia eupatoria)*
Bee Orchid *(Ophrys apifera)*
Black Medick *(Medicago lupulina)*
Bluebell (*Hyacinthoides non-scripta*)
Bugle *(Ajuga reptans)*
Bulbous Buttercup *(Ranunculus bulbosus)*
Bush Vetch *(Vicia sepium)*
Cleavers, Sticky Willy *(Galium aparine)*
Common Bird's-foot-trefoil, Eggs-and-Bacon *(Lotus corniculatus)*
Common Centaury *(Centaurium erythraea)*
Common Dog-violet *(Viola riviniana)*
Common Figwort *(Scrophularia nodosa)*
Common Knapweed, Hardheads (*Centaurea nigra)*
Common Milkwort *(Polygala vulgaris)*
Common Rock-rose *(Helianthemum nummularium)*
Common Spotted-orchid *(Dactylorhiza fuchsii)*
Common Twayblade *(Listera ovata)*
Common Valerian *(Valeriana officinalis)*
Cow Parsley, Queen Anne's Lace (*Anthriscus sylvestris)*
Cowslip *(Primula veris)*
Creeping Thistle *(Cirsium arvense)*
Crosswort *(Cruciata laevipes)*
Dewberry *(Rubus caesius)*
Dog's Mercury *(Mercurialis perennis)*
Dove's-foot Crane's-bill *(Geranium molle)*
Early Dog-violet *(Viola reichenbachiana)*

Early-purple Orchid *(Orchis mascula)*
Enchanter's-nightshade *(Circaea lutetiana)*
Eyebright *(Euphrasia officinalis agg.)*
Fairy Flax *(Linum catharticum)*
False Oxlip *(Primula vulgaris x veris)*
Fly Orchid *(Ophrys insectifera)*
Foxglove *(Digitalis purpurea)*
Garlic Mustard *(Alliaria petiolata)*
Goat's-beard *(Tragopogon pratensis ssp. minor)*
Greater Butterfly-orchid (*Platanthera chlorantha)*
Greater Stitchwort *(Stellaria holostea)*
Heath Bedstraw *(Galium saxatile)*
Heath Speedwell *(Veronica officinalis)*
Herb-Paris *(Paris quadrifolia)*
Herb-Robert *(Geranium robertianum)*
Hoary Plantain *(Plantago media)*
Hogweed *(Heracleum sphondylium)*
Horseshoe Vetch *(Hippocrepis comosa)*
Lady's Bedstraw *(Galium verum)*
Lesser Stitchwort *(Stellaria graminea)*
Lesser Trefoil *(Trifolium dubium)*
Marsh Thistle *(Cirsium palustre)*
Meadowsweet *(Filipendula ulmaria)*
Meadow Vetchling *(Lathyrus pratensis)*
Mouse-ear-hawkweed *(Pilosella officinarum)*
Nipplewort *(Lapsana communis)*
Oxeye Daisy *(Leucanthemum vulgare)*
Pignut *(Conopodium majus)*
Pineappleweed *(Matricaria discoidea)*
Primrose *(Primula vulgaris)*
Pyramidal Orchid *(Anacamptis pyramidalis)*
Ramsons *(Allium ursinum)*
Red Campion *(Silene dioica)*

Rough Chervil *(Chaerophyllum temulum)*
Salad Burnet *(Sanguisorba minor* ssp. *minor)*
Sanicle *(Sanicula europaea)*
Selfheal *(Prunella vulgaris)*
Sheep's Sorrel *(Rumex acetosella)*
Shepherd's-purse *(Capsella bursa-pastoris)*
Shining Crane's-bill *(Geranium lucidum)*
Small Scabious *(Scabiosa columbaria)*
Spear Thistle *(Cirsium vulgare)*
Squinancywort *(Asperula cynanchica)*

Three-nerved Sandwort *(Moehringia trinervia)*
Toothwort *(Lathraea squamaria)*
Wild Rose *(Rosa agg.)*
Wild Strawberry *(Fragaria vesca)*
Wild Thyme *(Thymus polytrichus)*
Wood Avens, Herb Bennet *(Geum urbanum)*
Woodruff *(Galium odoratum)*
Wood Sage *(Teucrium scorodonia)*
Wood Speedwell *(Veronica montana)*
Yarrow *(Achillea millefolium)*
Yellow Archangel *(Lamiastrum galeobdolon)*

Below: *A five-leaved Herb-Paris*

WALK 5

HOUND'S-TONGUE AND
HORSESHOE VETCH IN PURBECK
Ballard Down

A late spring walk near Swanage. Starting at a lay-by on the outskirts of the town, we make our way to the top of Ballard Down past a delightful variety of chalk-loving flowers. From the summit we have majestic views of Poole Harbour, Studland Bay, and, on a clear day, the Isle of Wight.

We then enjoy an exhilarating walk along the ridge of the Down, before descending to the lay-by past large patches of Horseshoe Vetch.

Time of year:	early May to late June
Distance:	about 1¾ miles (3 km)
Difficulty:	fairly strenuous with steep hills
Parking:	large lay-by off Swanage to Studland road at SZ 022 809 (free)
Directions to parking area:	take the A351 to Swanage. Turn left at the sea front (signposted "Studland Poole & Bournemouth via toll ferry"). Continue for nearly 1½ miles (2½ km) until you reach the first of two lay-bys on your right, shortly after passing 40 mph speed limit signs.
Ordnance Survey maps:	1:50,000 Landranger 195 Bournemouth & Purbeck 1:25,000 Explorer OL 15 Purbeck & South Dorset
Public transport:	50 bus between Bournemouth and Swanage stops close to lay-by (check timetable)
Refreshments:	in Swanage
Toilets:	none

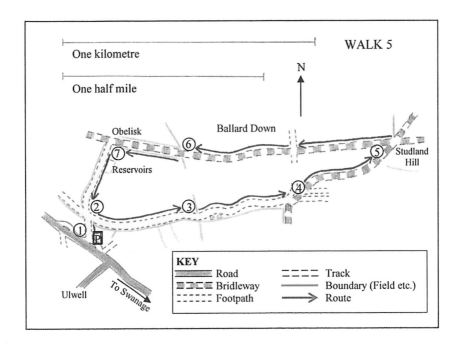

ROUTE

1. Leave the lay-by through a kissing gate next to a sign for a footpath. Continue straight ahead on the footpath (roughly north) uphill for 100 yards (90 metres) until it is crossed by another footpath at a marker stone. *Bladder Campion, Common Gromwell, Crosswort, Hound's-tongue and Vervain are found in the scrubby area around the stone.*

2. Turn right (roughly south-east) on to this footpath (indicated on the marker stone "to Coast Path"). Continue on the footpath (roughly south-east then east) gradually uphill for 550 yards (500 metres) until you reach a stile, waymarked "Purbeck Way", at a National Trust sign for Ballard Down. As you proceed there are attractive views of Godlingston Hill behind you. *To your left is a profusion of chalk-loving flowers, including Common Rock-rose, Crosswort, Greater Knapweed, Hound's-tongue, Long-stalked Crane's-bill, Weld and Wild Marjoram. There are also large areas of Horseshoe Vetch, where in mid- to late May you may see the beautiful Adonis Blue butterfly.*

Horseshoe Vetch

Usually at its best in May, Horseshoe Vetch is found in great numbers on the sunny southern slopes of Ballard Down, covering the ground in large brilliant yellow patches.

The flowers are about ½ inch (1¼ cm) long, shaped like other members of the pea family, and grow in long-stalked heads. Bright yellow with reddish brown veins, they have a heady perfume, which is particularly strong in warm weather. After flowering, they form a pod which eventually breaks up into horseshoe-shaped parts, giving the plant its name. The leaves are divided into about 4-5 pairs of tiny, well-separated leaflets with a single leaflet at the tip.

Horseshoe Vetch is widespread in Dorset in short chalk and limestone turf, especially on warm south-facing slopes. It is the foodplant of the caterpillars of the Adonis Blue butterfly and, if you visit Ballard Down on a sunny day in mid- to late May, you may see the brilliant turquoise blue male butterflies flying around the plants.

3. Cross the stile and continue (east) on the footpath for 450 yards (410 metres), until it is crossed by a bridleway. As you go along you will have excellent views over Swanage Bay to your right (roughly south).
    Shortly before the crossing, the tall spikes of Milk Thistle may be seen to the right of the footpath.
4. Turn left (roughly north-east) on to the bridleway (indicated on a marker stone "Studland") and follow it uphill, passing a stone bench on your left after a few yards.
    Common Rock-rose, Eyebright, Squinancywort, Weld and Wild Thyme grow beside the bridleway.
    Continue on the bridleway (generally north-east) up the hill for 550 yards (500 metres) until it is crossed by another bridleway at the top close to a marker stone.

Opposite*: A bank of Horseshoe Vetch.*

5.   Turn left (roughly west) on to this bridleway (indicated on the marker stone "The Obelisk") and continue for ½ mile (800 metres) until you reach a gate waymarked for a bridleway "The National Trust". There are magnificent views to your right (north) of Poole Harbour and Studland Bay, while behind you (east) are the chalk cliffs of the Isle of Wight.

6.   Go through the gate and continue on the bridleway (roughly west) slightly downhill for 300 yards (275 metres) until you reach the obelisk on your right with a stile, waymarked for a footpath "The National Trust", on your left.

    In the field in front of you clumps of Crosswort grow with Germander Speedwell (see painting on page 55).

7.   Turn left and cross the stile on to the footpath (indicated on a marker stone "Ulwell"); continue (roughly south) on the footpath, which soon takes you down a long flight of steps, until after 300 yards (275 metres) you reach the crossing where you turned right at stage 2. Continue straight ahead at the crossing and retrace your steps to the lay-by.

    There are large patches of Horseshoe Vetch to the left of the steps.

Opposite: *Milk Thistle, usually found close to the sea.*

Below: *View from the summit of Ballard Down to the north.*

"...silver sunbeams lighted up a many-armed inland sea which stretched round an island with fir-trees and gorse, and amid brilliant crimson heaths wherein white paths and roads occasionally met the eye in dashes and zig-zags like flashes of lightning."

From *The Hand of Ethelberta*,
Thomas Hardy

Hound's-tongue

Hound's-tongue can be found scattered over Ballard Down, most frequently in scrubby areas on its lower slopes.

The plants are usually about 2½ feet (75 cm) tall and noticeably upright, the flowers growing in branched one-sided spikes on leafy stems. The individual flowers are just over ¼ inch (6 mm) across and have 5 beautifully veined maroon or purplish deep blue petals, joined at the base. After each flower fades, a fruit of 4 bristly nutlets appears in its place.

The narrow, pointed greyish leaves are softly hairy and sufficiently like a dog's tongue to give the plant its name. They have a strong, distinctive smell, usually described as being like mice, but also, less commonly, roasted peanuts!

Hound's-tongue is uncommon in Dorset, being mostly confined to coastal areas and the north-east: it is usually found in chalky grassland or at the back of beaches. It has declined over the past 50 years, both here and in Britain as a whole, probably due to the use of intensive farming methods.

Left below*: The bristly fruit of Hound's-tongue.*

Some of the flowers you may see on this walk

Agrimony *(Agrimonia eupatoria)*
Bastard-toadflax *(Thesium humifusum)*
Bittersweet, Woody Nightshade
    (Solanum dulcamara)
Black Medick *(Medicago lupulina)*
Black Horehound *(Ballota nigra)*
Bladder Campion *(Silene vulgaris)*
Bristly Oxtongue *(Picris echioides)*
Bulbous Buttercup *(Ranunculus
    bulbosus)*
Cat's-ear *(Hypochaeris radicata)*
Changing Forget-me-not *(Myosotis
    discolor)*
Common Bird's-foot-trefoil, Eggs-and-
    Bacon *(Lotus corniculatus)*
Common Centaury *(Centaurium
    erythraea)*
Common Field-speedwell *(Veronica
    persica)*
Common Gromwell *(Lithospermum
    officinale)*
Common Mallow *(Malva sylvestris)*
Common Milkwort *(Polygala vulgaris)*
Common Restharrow *(Ononis repens)*
Common Rock-rose *(Helianthemum
    nummularium)*
Common Vetch *(Vicia sativa)*
Cowslip *(Primula veris)*
Creeping Cinquefoil *(Potentilla
    reptans)*
Crosswort *(Cruciata laevipes)*
Dove's-foot Crane's-bill *(Geranium
    molle)*
Eyebright *(Euphrasia officinalis agg.)*
Fairy Flax *(Linum catharticum)*
Field Bindweed *(Convolvulus arvensis)*
Field Scabious *(Knautia arvensis)*
Germander Speedwell *(Veronica
    chamaedrys)*

Right above:
*Weld on the
lower slopes
of Ballard
Down.*

Right:
Vervain

Below:
*Common
Gromwell*

Goat's-beard *(Tragopogon pratensis* ssp. *minor)*
Gorse *(Ulex europaeus)*
Greater Knapweed *(Centaurea scabiosa)*
Great Mullein *(Verbascum thapsus)*
Hedge Bedstraw *(Galium mollugo)*
Herb-Robert *(Geranium robertianum)*
Hoary Plantain *(Plantago media)*
Hogweed *(Heracleum sphondylium)*
Hop Trefoil *(Trifolium campestre)*
Horseshoe Vetch *(Hippocrepis comosa)*
Hound's-tongue *(Cynoglossum officinale)*
Kidney Vetch *(Anthyllis vulneraria)*
Knotted Hedge-parsley *(Torilis nodosa)*
Lady's Bedstraw *(Galium verum)*
Lesser Centaury *(Centaurium pulchellum)*
Lesser Trefoil *(Trifolium dubium)*
Long-stalked Crane's-bill *(Geranium columbinum)*
Meadow Vetchling *(Lathyrus pratensis)*
Milk Thistle *(Silybum marianum)*
Mouse-ear-hawkweed *(Pilosella officinarum)*
Musk Thistle, Nodding Thistle *(Carduus nutans)*
Nipplewort *(Lapsana communis)*
Oxeye Daisy *(Leucanthemum vulgare)*
Pale Flax *(Linum bienne)*
Parsley-piert *(Aphanes arvensis)*
Perforate St. John's-wort *(Hypericum perforatum)*

Pyramidal Orchid *(Anacamptis pyramidalis)*
Red Campion *(Silene dioica)*
Rough Chervil *(Chaerophyllum temulum)*
Salad Burnet *(Sanguisorba minor* ssp. *minor)*
Scarlet Pimpernel *(Anagallis arvensis* ssp. *arvensis)*
Selfheal *(Prunella vulgaris)*
Sheep's Sorrel *(Rumex acetosella)*
Slender Thistle *(Carduus tenuiflorus)*
Small-flowered Buttercup *(Ranunculus parviflorus)*
Spear Thistle *(Cirsium vulgare)*
Squinancywort *(Asperula cynanchica)*
Stinking Iris, Gladdon *(Iris foetidissima)*
Thyme-leaved Speedwell *(Veronica serpyllifolia)*
Vervain *(Verbena officinalis)*
Wall Speedwell *(Veronica arvensis)*
Weld *(Reseda luteola)*
White Campion *(Silene latifolia)*
Wild Carrot *(Daucus carota* ssp. *carota)*
Wild Marjoram *(Origanum vulgare)*
Wild Parsnip *(Pastinaca sativa* var. *sativa)*
Wild Privet *(Ligustrum vulgare)*
Wild Rose *(Rosa agg.)*
Wild Thyme *(Thymus polytrichus)*
Wood Sage *(Teucrium scorodonia)*
Yarrow *(Achillea millefolium)*
Yellow-wort *(Blackstonia perfoliata)*

Opposite: Crosswort and Germander Speedwell

WALK 6

ORCHIDS ON AN EAST DORSET
IRON AGE HILL-FORT
Badbury Rings

An early summer walk near Wimborne Minster. We start along the banks of Badbury Rings, seeing a magnificent display of orchids and other chalk-loving flowers.

From the Rings we take a bridleway to the Wimborne Minster to Blandford road. We then follow another bridleway parallel to the road, beside an avenue of beech trees sheltering the beautiful White Helleborine, before returning to our starting point along the path of a Roman road.

Time of year:	late May to mid-July
Distance:	about 2 miles (3¼ km) short route: about 1¼ miles (2 km)
Difficulty:	both routes easy
Parking:	National Trust car park at ST 960 030 (free) [narrow entrance: maximum width 2.4 metres]
Directions to car park:	from Wimborne Minster take the B3082 north-west towards Blandford. Pass the entrance to Kingston Lacy House on your left and continue for 1½ miles (2½ km) until you reach a right turn signposted " Badbury Rings", almost opposite a left turn signposted " Shapwick". Turn right up a track and continue for 250 yards (230 metres) until you reach the car park.
Ordnance Survey maps:	1:50,000 Landranger 195 Bournemouth & Purbeck 1:25,000 Explorer 118 Shaftesbury & Cranborne Chase
Public transport:	none
Refreshments:	in Wimborne Minster
Toilets:	none

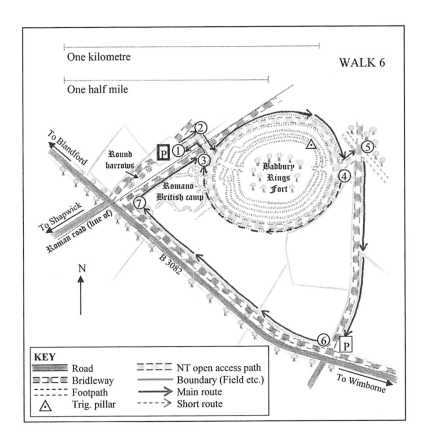

ROUTE

Please note that dogs are not permitted on the Rings.

1. Leave the car park at the far right (north-east) end from where you entered, through a gap in bushes leading to a kissing gate. There is an interesting National Trust information board by the kissing gate. Go through the gate on to a footpath and follow it (roughly north-east) for 40 yards (35 metres) until you reach another kissing gate.

2. Go through the kissing gate and make your way towards the gap in the banks ahead of you (roughly south-east) until after 100 yards (90 metres) you reach the outermost bank.

3. Turn left (roughly north-east), climb on to the top of the bank and continue in a semi-circle (roughly north-east, then east, south-east and south) for just under ½ mile (750 metres) until you reach a gap in the bank with a footpath on your left leading to a stile with woodland beyond. As you walk round, Cranborne Chase (see Walk 1) can be seen in the distance to the north while, just before you reach the gap, the white cliffs of the Isle of Wight are visible to the south-east on a clear day.

   There is a wonderful display of wild flowers along the sides of the bank, including Chalk Milkwort (with bright blue, pink or white flowers), Common Spotted-, Fragrant, Frog, Greater Butterfly- and Pyramidal Orchids, Common Twayblade, Squinancywort, Wild Thyme and Yellow-rattle.

4. Descend from the bank, turn sharply left (roughly north-east) on to the footpath and continue for 100 yards (90 metres) until you reach the stile.

   Sanicle can be found close to the stile.

5. Cross the stile and turn right (south) on to a bridleway. Continue (generally south) for ½ mile (800 metres) until you reach a crossing bridleway at a small car park off the B3082 Wimborne Minster to Blandford road.

   Bladder Campion, Field Scabious, Greater Knapweed and Long-stalked Crane's-bill grow beside the bridleway.

Below: *Badbury Rings from the east.*

Badbury Rings

"Above this place is the great fort of Badbury Rings, and it is worth while to visit Dorset, if for no other purpose than to see this romantic spot."

From *Highways and Byways in Dorset*,
Sir Frederick Treves

With three rings of banks and ditches surrounding a wooded hill top, Badbury Rings is a most impressive Iron Age hill-fort and indeed worth a long journey to see!

Although now uninhabited, the area saw a great deal of human activity both before and after the construction of the Rings over 2,000 years ago. The three round barrows you see close to the car park are probably Bronze Age, dating from around 2,000 BC, while, close by, the path of a Roman road from Old Sarum to Dorchester and the remains of a small Romano-British camp are visible (see map page 57). The road crossed another, running from Bath to Hamworthy, just north of the Rings and so the area must have been a centre of activity in Roman times.

The Rings are home to an outstanding variety of wild flowers, many of which grow in great profusion. The chalky soil naturally supports a large number of flower species, but they have survived because the area has escaped ploughing and the use of fertilisers and weedkillers. At the same time, regular grazing has helped to protect the many small and delicate plants from being overrun by stronger-growing vegetation.

As a result, you can see many different species of orchids here, including Bee, Common Spotted-, Early-purple, Fragrant, Frog (see page 60), Greater Butterfly- and Pyramidal, as well as other attractive flowers such as Bastard-toadflax, Chalk Milkwort, Dwarf Thistle, Horseshoe Vetch (see page 48), Salad Burnet, Squinancywort and Wild Thyme.

".... Nature has pressed all these ages of man, those of peace and of war, into one harmonious masterpiece where contemporary man, slipping for a moment out of the clutch of his own age, ... may drink deep of a unity and repose transcending time itself."

From *English Downland*,
H. J. Massingham

Frog Orchid

Frog Orchid is found in small groups here and there on closely-grazed banks of Badbury Rings.

Visible from around the end of June, the plants are up to about 6 inches (15 cm) tall - although often shorter - and have a loose spike of flowers at the top of the stem. The flowers are greenish, tinged with red, and about ¼ inch (6 mm) across. The lip, shaped like a curved strap with a forked tip, is often bent back, while above is a hood of petals and sepals. The flower is said, with some imagination, to resemble a jumping frog! The upper leaves are narrow and pointed, clasping the stem, while the lower are broader and form a rosette at the base.

The small size and inconspicuous colouring of the plants make them difficult to find, but, after spotting one you often see several more, as your eyes become used to separating the small spikes from their grassy background.

Frog Orchid is scarce in Dorset, being found mostly in short chalk turf in the north-east of the county. It has declined here in recent years, probably due to reduced levels of grazing and the invasion of scrub. Decreases have also been seen in Britain as a whole, although it remains quite common in parts of Scotland.

6. Turn right on to this bridleway and continue parallel to the road (roughly north-west) for nearly ¾ mile (just over 1 km) until you reach a wooden gate on your right, waymarked for a bridleway, at the track you took to the main car park.
   About halfway along, the beautiful White Helleborine, usually at its best in late May or early June, grows under the avenue of beech trees beside the road, while Bee Orchid and Hedgerow Crane's-bill may be found by the bridleway.

7. Turn right, go through the gate on to the bridleway and follow it (roughly north-east) for ¼ mile (400 metres) along the path of a Roman road, passing three round barrows on your left, until you see on your left the kissing gate you went through at stage 2. There is an excellent view of the Rings from the bridleway.
   Retrace your steps to the car park.
   Chalk Milkwort, Common Knapweed, Kidney Vetch, Salad Burnet and Wild Mignonette grow close to the bridleway.

Opposite: *Frog Orchids*

SHORT ROUTE

(a) Follow the main route to the end of stage 3.

(b) Cross the gap and climb on to the top of the outermost bank on the other side. Continue in a semi-circle (roughly south, then south-west, west, north-west, north and north-east) for just over ½ mile (nearly 1 km) until you reach the gap where you joined the bank at the start of stage 3.
There is a fine display of orchids and other attractive flowers, such as Agrimony, Bastard-toadflax, Common Valerian, Kidney Vetch and Squinancywort, along the bank.

(c) Retrace your steps to the car park.

Opposite: *Fragrant Orchids*
Above: *Common Spotted-orchids*
Below: *Wild Thyme*

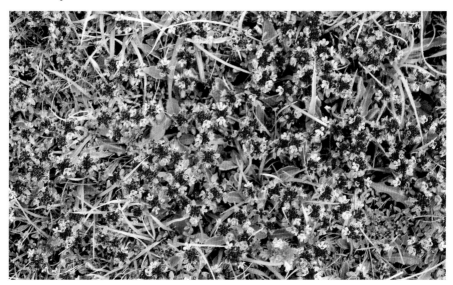

White Helleborine

You can find White Helleborine under the magnificent avenue of beech trees lining the Wimborne Minster to Blandford road. The trees were planted in 1835, with one for every day of the year on each side of the road.

The plants are usually about 9 inches (23 cm) tall, with a short spike of flowers at the top of a leafy stem. Each flower is about ¾ inch (2 cm) long, creamy white and roughly oval, giving the plant its old name of Egg Orchid. They rarely open fully, although a patch of pale orange in the centre can sometimes be glimpsed through the partly opened sepals and petals. The flowers are usually at their best in late May or early June.

The leaves are greyish green and strongly veined; narrow and pointed near the top of the stem and broader lower down, they hold themselves elegantly beneath the flowers.

This most graceful plant, a member of the orchid family, is usually found in Dorset under beech trees on chalky soils. It has declined both here and in other parts of England over the past century, perhaps due to the clearance of woodland.

Opposite: White Helleborine

Right: Greater Butterfly-orchid

Below: Squinancywort

Some of the flowers you may see on this walk

Agrimony *(Agrimonia eupatoria)*
Bastard-toadflax *(Thesium humifusum)*
Beaked Hawk's-beard *(Crepis vesicaria)*
Bee Orchid *(Ophrys apifera)*
Bittersweet, Woody Nightshade *(Solanum dulcamara)*
Black Bryony (*Tamus communis*)
Black Horehound *(Ballota nigra)*
Black Medick *(Medicago lupulina)*
Bladder Campion (*Silene vulgaris*)
Bulbous Buttercup *(Ranunculus bulbosus)*
Carline Thistle *(Carlina vulgaris)*
Chalk Milkwort *(Polygala calcarea)*
Common Bird's-foot-trefoil, Eggs-and-Bacon *(Lotus corniculatus)*
Common Knapweed, Hardheads *(Centaurea nigra)*
Common Milkwort *(Polygala vulgaris)*
Common Spotted-orchid *(Dactylorhiza fuchsii)*
Common Restharrow *(Ononis repens)*
Common Twayblade *(Listera ovata)*
Common Valerian *(Valeriana officinalis)*
Common Vetch *(Vicia sativa)*
Cowslip *(Primula veris)*
Creeping Cinquefoil *(Potentilla reptans)*
Cut-leaved Crane's-bill *(Geranium dissectum)*
Dove's-foot Crane's-bill *(Geranium molle)*
Dwarf Thistle, Stemless Thistle *(Cirsium acaule)*
Early-purple Orchid *(Orchis mascula)*
Eyebright *(Euphrasia officinalis agg.)*

Fairy Flax *(Linum cartharticum)*
Field Bindweed *(Convolvulus arvensis)*
Field Forget-me-not *(Myosotis arvensis)*
Field Scabious *(Knautia arvensis)*
Fragrant Orchid *(Gymnadenia conopsea)*
Frog Orchid *(Coeloglossum viride)*
Germander Speedwell *(Veronica chamaedrys)*
Goat's-beard *(Tragopogon pratensis ssp. minor)*
Great Mullein *(Verbascum thapsus)*
Greater Butterfly-orchid (*Platanthera chlorantha*)
Greater Knapweed *(Centaurea scabiosa)*
Hedge Bedstraw *(Galium mollugo)*
Hedgerow Crane's-bill *(Geranium pyrenaicum)*
Hemlock *(Conium maculatum)*
Hemp-agrimony *(Eupatorium cannabinum)*
Herb-Robert *(Geranium robertianum)*
Hoary Plantain *(Plantago media)*
Hogweed *(Heracleum sphondylium)*
Hop Trefoil *(Trifolium campestre)*
Horseshoe Vetch *(Hippocrepis comosa)*
Kidney Vetch *(Anthyllis vulneraria)*
Lady's Bedstraw *(Galium verum)*
Lesser Trefoil *(Trifolium dubium)*
Long-stalked Crane's-bill *(Geranium columbinum)*
Marsh Thistle *(Cirsium palustre)*
Meadow Buttercup *(Ranunculus acris)*
Meadow Vetchling *(Lathyrus pratensis)*
Mouse-ear-hawkweed *(Pilosella officinarum)*

Musk Thistle, Nodding Thistle
 (Carduus nutans)
Nipplewort *(Lapsana communis)*
Oxeye Daisy *(Leucanthemum vulgare)*
Perennial Sow-thistle *(Sonchus arvensis)*
Perforate St. John's-wort *(Hypericum perforatum)*
Prickly Sow-thistle *(Sonchus asper)*
Pyramidal Orchid *(Anacamptis pyramidalis)*
Red Bartsia *(Odontites vernus)*
Red Campion *(Silene dioica)*
Rough Chervil *(Chaerophyllum temulum)*
Salad Burnet *(Sanguisorba minor* ssp. *minor)*
Sanicle *(Sanicula europaea)*
Selfheal *(Prunella vulgaris)*
Small Scabious *(Scabiosa columbaria)*
Spear Thistle *(Cirsium vulgare)*
Squinancywort *(Asperula cynanchica)*
Stinking Iris, Gladdon *(Iris foetidissima)*

Tufted Vetch *(Vicia cracca)*
Upright Hedge-parsley *(Torilis japonica)*
Weld *(Reseda luteola)*
Welted Thistle *(Carduus crispus)*
White Bryony *(Bryonia dioica)*
White Campion *(Silene latifolia)*
White Helleborine *(Cephalanthera damasonium)*
Wild Basil *(Clinopodium vulgare)*
Wild Carrot *(Daucus carota* ssp. *carota)*
Wild Mignonette *(Reseda lutea)*
Wild Parsnip *(Pastinaca sativa* var. *sativa)*
Wild Privet *(Ligustrum vulgare)*
Wild Rose *(Rosa agg.)*
Wild Thyme *(Thymus polytrichus)*
Yarrow *(Achillea millefolium)*
Yellow-rattle *(Rhinanthus minor)*

Right: Common Twayblade
Below: Yellow-rattle

WALK 7

SUMMER FLOWERS ON CHALK CLIFFS
White Nothe

A midsummer walk along chalk cliffs on the coast east of Weymouth. Starting on downland overlooking Portland, we take a track downhill to join the coast path. We then follow the path eastwards along cliff tops to White Nothe, where we find many attractive flowers. We continue on the coast path close to cliff tops rich in chalk-loving flowers, before turning inland and returning to the car park over farmland.

On a clear day we have magnificent views of the coast and sea throughout the walk.

Please keep well away from all cliff edges.

Time of year:	late May to mid-July
Distance:	about 3½ miles (5¾ km)
Difficulty:	fairly strenuous with some steep hills
Parking:	National Trust car park at SY 759 824 (free)
Directions to car park:	from Dorchester take the A352 towards Wareham. Pass through Broadmayne and continue for 1¼ miles (2 km) until you reach a roundabout. Turn right at the roundabout on to the A353 (signposted "Weymouth"). Pass through Poxwell, and, just after a sharp right bend, take the first turn on your left (signposted "Ringstead 1½"). Continue for 1¼ miles (2 km), ignoring a right turn (signposted "Ringstead Bay and Beach"), until you reach the car park.
Ordnance Survey maps:	1:50,000 Landranger 194 Dorchester & Weymouth 1:25,000 Explorer OL 15 Purbeck & South Dorset
Public transport:	none
Refreshments:	none
Toilets:	none

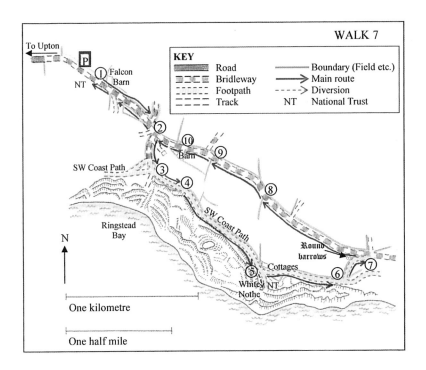

ROUTE

1. Leave the car park by the gate at the east end (the opposite end from where you drove in). From the car park you have a superb view of Portland to the south. Go through the gate on to a track and follow it downhill (roughly south-east) for 550 yards (500 metres) where it turns sharply right immediately beyond a National Trust sign for Ringstead Bay.

2. Follow the track round to the right (roughly south) and continue downhill for 300 yards (275 metres), ignoring a road running off to the right after 200 yards (180 metres), until you reach a stile on your left where the coast path crosses the track.

3. Turn left (signposted "White Nothe ¾") and cross the stile into a field, joining the coast path, which you will be following until stage 6. Continue on the coast path (roughly south-east) uphill across the field for 400 yards (360 metres) until you reach a kissing gate at the top. From the top there is a good view behind you (roughly west) towards Ringstead and Weymouth. *Slender, Spear and Marsh Thistles all grow in this field.*

Viper's-bugloss

As you walk along the coast path you will see the striking blue spikes of Viper's-bugloss scattered along the cliff tops.

The spikes are up to about 2½ feet (75 cm) tall and bear the brilliant blue funnel-shaped flowers in small sprays. The individual flowers are about ½ inch (1¼ cm) across and have 5 unequal petal lobes, giving them a rather unusual appearance. With pink buds and long purple stamens protruding from the mouth of the flowers, the plants stand out vividly against the white cliffs. The greyish leaves are narrow and pointed and grow around the lower stems; both the leaves and stems are bristly.

"Viper's" in the plant's name reflects the resemblance of the fruit and stems to an adder's head and skin respectively, while "bugloss" comes from the Greek word for ox-tongue and refers to the rough, tongue-shaped leaves.

Viper's-bugloss is fairly frequent in Dorset on chalk and limestone cliffs; it is also found inland on dry sandy or chalky soils. This most attractive flower is fairly widespread in England, Wales and the South of Scotland.

Opposite: *Viper's-bugloss above Ringstead Bay.*

4. Go through the kissing gate and continue on the coast path (generally south-east) for ½ mile (800 metres), keeping well away from the cliff edge on your right, until you reach a row of old coastguard cottages. As you go along you have excellent views of the chalk cliff of White Nothe ahead of you and of the undercliff, formed by landslips, below you to your right. *Common Restharrow, Goat's-beard, Lady's Bedstraw, Nottingham Catchfly (sometimes abundant), Stinking Iris, Viper's-bugloss and Wild Thyme are found to the right of the path.*

5. Go past the cottages and continue on the coast path (roughly east) for 700 yards (640 metres), keeping well away from the cliff edge on the right, until you reach a kissing gate on your left, waymarked for a footpath, with a stone indicating "Daggers Gate South Down NT" close by. There are magnificent views ahead (roughly east) along the chalk cliffs towards Bat's Head, Durdle Door, and, seen in the distance on a clear day, St. Aldhelm's Head. *In early July, the cliff top here has a stunning array of chalk-loving wild flowers, including Greater Knapweed, Ploughman's-spikenard, Pyramidal Orchid, Small Scabious, Viper's-bugloss, Wild Marjoram and Wild Thyme.*

White Nothe

"As a child I had been taught to refer to the cliff as the White Nore; on the other hand the gate of the coastguard station through which I passed every day presented my eyes with the words White Nothe; while the people of Chaldon Herring were all of them confident that I was living at White Nose. It was this last judgement which eventually won emphatic confirmation from the late Mr. Thomas Hardy, who said: "Of course it is White Nose, it always has been called White Nose. You can see if you look that the cliff is shaped like a nose. It is like the Duke of Wellington's nose." "

From *Dorset Essays*,
Llewelyn Powys

Whichever name is correct, at about 500 feet the cliff is the highest for miles around and a prominent landmark from Weymouth.

To walk round the summit, turn half right (roughly south-east) on to a grassy footpath (indicated on a stone marker "White Nothe"), when you reach the row of old coastguard cottages at the end of stage 4. Llewelyn Powys and his wife lived in one of these cottages for several years. Continue on this path for just over 100 yards (90 metres) until you reach a Second World War building on your right. Retrace your steps to the cottages when you wish to rejoin the route.

From the summit there are outstanding views to the south-west and west (on your right as you face the sea) of Portland and Weymouth Bay, while on a clear day you can see in the distance St. Catherine's Chapel at Abbotsbury (see Walk 3) and, to its right, Hardy's Monument. To the east there is perhaps an even better view along the line of chalk cliffs, with Bat's Head in the middle distance and, visible on a clear day, the flat shape of St. Aldhelm's Head far beyond.

There is a good variety of chalk-loving flowers on the summit, including Common Rock-rose, Horseshoe Vetch (see page 48), Pyramidal Orchid, Shaggy Mouse-ear-hawkweed, Squinancywort and Viper's-bugloss (see page 70), while the influence of the sea is felt near the cliff edge where Rock Samphire, Sea Beet and Wild Cabbage can be seen.

Opposite*: White Nothe from the north-west.*

6. Turn left and go through the kissing gate into a field, leaving the coast path. Follow the footpath along the left edge of the field (roughly north-east) for 220 yards (200 metres) where it turns sharply right at the corner, close to two round barrows. Continue on the footpath (roughly east) for a further 75 yards (70 metres) until you reach a stone marker (indicating "Coast Path ¼ White Nose ½ Daggers Gate 1¾"). There is a memorial stone to Llewelyn Powys 350 yards (320 metres) east of this point.

    Shortly after you go through the kissing gate, Long-stalked Crane's-bill can be seen on your left.

7. Go to the other side of the stone marker, where you will see indicated a bridleway to "South Down 1½ Ringstead 2¼". Take this bridleway (roughly west - almost reversing your previous direction of travel), going through the smaller of two metal gates into the field beyond. As you pass through the gate you will see behind you an information board headed "Chaldon Down Visitors Information" describing the downland landscape. Follow the bridleway along the right edge of the field (roughly west then north-west) for just over ½ mile (nearly 1 km) until you reach a gate on the far side.

    Field Bindweed and Scentless Mayweed (see painting on page 77), together with Dwarf Spurge, Field Pansy and Wall Speedwell, may be found in this field.

8. Go through the gate into the next field and follow the bridleway along its right edge (roughly north then north-west) for 600 yards (550 metres) until you reach a gate on the far side.

9. Go through the gate and continue to follow the bridleway along the right edge of the next field (roughly north-west) for 150 yards (135 metres) until you reach a gate on the far side.

10. Go through the gate and follow the bridleway straight ahead (roughly north-west), passing a thatched barn on your left, until, after 350 yards (320 metres), you reach the track you followed in stages 1 & 2. Join the track and retrace your steps to the car park.

Some of the flowers you may see on this walk

Betony *(Stachys officinalis)*
Bladder Campion *(Silene vulgaris)*
Bristly Oxtongue *(Picris echioides)*
Bugloss *(Anchusa arvensis)*
Bulbous Buttercup *(Ranunculus bulbosus)*
Common Bird's-foot-trefoil, Eggs-and-Bacon *(Lotus corniculatus)*
Common Centaury *(Centaurium erythraea)*
Common Field-speedwell *(Veronica persica)*
Common Knapweed, Hardheads *(Centaurea nigra)*
Common Mallow *(Malva sylvestris)*
Common Milkwort *(Polygala vulgaris)*
Common Restharrow *(Ononis repens)*
Common Rock-rose *(Helianthemum nummularium)*
Creeping Thistle *(Cirsium arvense)*
Dame's-violet *(Hesperis matronalis)*
Dove's-foot Crane's-bill *(Geranium molle)*
Dwarf Spurge *(Euphorbia exigua)*
Dwarf Thistle, Stemless Thistle *(Cirsium acaule)*
Fairy Flax *(Linum catharticum)*

Field Bindweed *(Convolvulus arvensis)*
Field Madder *(Sherardia arvensis)*
Field Pansy *(Viola arvensis)*
Field Scabious *(Knautia arvensis)*
Foxglove *(Digitalis purpurea)*
Great Lettuce *(Lactuca virosa)*
Great Willowherb *(Epilobium hirsutum)*
Germander Speedwell *(Veronica chamaedrys)*
Goat's-beard *(Tragopogon pratensis* ssp. *minor)*
Greater Knapweed *(Centaurea scabiosa)*
Greater Plantain *(Plantago major)*
Harebell *(Campanula rotundifolia)*
Hedge Bedstraw *(Galium mollugo)*
Hoary Plantain *(Plantago media)*

Opposite*: Opium Poppy*
Below left*: Wild Carrot*
Below right*: Nottingham Catchfly*

Horseshoe Vetch *(Hippocrepis comosa)*
Kidney Vetch *(Anthyllis vulneraria)*
Lady's Bedstraw *(Galium verum)*
Lesser Burdock *(Arctium minus)*
Lesser Stitchwort *(Stellaria graminea)*
Long-stalked Crane's-bill *(Geranium columbinum)*
Marsh Thistle *(Cirsium palustre)*
Meadow Vetchling *(Lathyrus pratensis)*
Milk Thistle *(Silybum marianum)*
Musk Thistle, Nodding Thistle *(Carduus nutans)*
Nottingham Catchfly *(Silene nutans)*
Opium Poppy *(Papaver somniferum)*
Oxeye Daisy *(Leucanthemum vulgare)*
Pignut *(Conopodium majus)*
Ploughman's-spikenard *(Inula conyzae)*
Portland Spurge *(Euphorbia portlandica)*
Purple Toadflax *(Linaria purpurea)*
Pyramidal Orchid *(Anacamptis pyramidalis)*
Red Valerian *(Centranthus ruber)*
Rosebay Willowherb *(Chamerion angustifolium)*
Salad Burnet *(Sanguisorba minor* ssp. *minor)*
Scarlet Pimpernel *(Anagallis arvensis* ssp. *arvensis)*
Scentless Mayweed *(Tripleurospermum inodorum)*
Sea Beet *(Beta vulgaris* ssp. *maritima)*

Shaggy Mouse-ear-hawkweed *(Pilosella peleteriana* ssp. *subpeleteriana)*
Sheep's Sorrel *(Rumex acetosella)*
Slender Thistle *(Carduus tenuiflorus)*
Slender Trefoil *(Trifolium micranthum)*
Small Scabious *(Scabiosa columbaria)*
Smooth Sow-thistle *(Sonchus oleraceus)*
Spear Thistle *(Cirsium vulgare)*
Squinancywort *(Asperula cynanchica)*
Stinking Iris, Gladdon *(Iris foetidissima)*
Thyme-leaved Speedwell *(Veronica serpyllifolia)*
Tufted Vetch *(Vicia cracca)*
Upright Hedge-parsley *(Torilis japonica)*
Viper's-bugloss *(Echium vulgare)*
Wall Speedwell *(Veronica arvensis)*
Weld *(Reseda luteola)*
Wild Cabbage, Sea Cabbage *(Brassica oleracea* var. *oleracea)*
Wild Carrot *(Daucus carota* ssp. *carota)*
Wild Marjoram *(Origanum vulgare)*
Wild Thyme *(Thymus polytrichus)*
Wild Madder *(Rubia peregrina)*
Wood Sage *(Teucrium scorodonia)*
Yarrow *(Achillea millefolium)*
Yellow-wort *(Blackstonia perfoliata)*

Opposite: *Field Bindweed twining itself around Scentless Mayweed.*

WALK 8

RIVER AND RAILWAY FLOWERS IN SUMMER
Fiddleford Manor and Mill

A midsummer walk along the River Stour and an old railway line near Sturminster Newton. Starting close to Fiddleford Manor, we cross the Stour at an old water mill and follow its banks to a rebuilt former railway bridge, seeing a variety of water plants.

We then continue along the line of the old railway, where we find an interesting mixture of wild flowers, before returning to the car park over farmland. We also have the opportunity to visit Fiddleford Manor to see its superb wooden roofs.

Please do not attempt this walk shortly after a long spell of heavy rain as the route may not be passable due to flooding.

Time of year:	late June to early August
Distance:	about 1¾ miles (3 km)
Difficulty:	easy but often muddy in places
Parking:	Fiddleford Manor car park at ST 802 135 (free)
Directions to car park:	from the traffic lights at Sturminster Newton Town Bridge take the A357 towards Blandford. After 1 mile (1½ km) take the first turn on your left (signposted "Fiddleford Manor"). The car park is on your left about 250 yards (230 metres) down the road.
Ordnance Survey maps:	1:50,000 Landranger 194 Dorchester & Weymouth 1:25,000 Explorer 129 Yeovil & Sherborne
Public transport:	310 bus between Sturminster Newton and Blandford and 368 bus between Yeovil and Blandford stop in Fiddleford village (check timetables)
Refreshments:	in Fiddleford village and Sturminster Newton
Toilets:	none

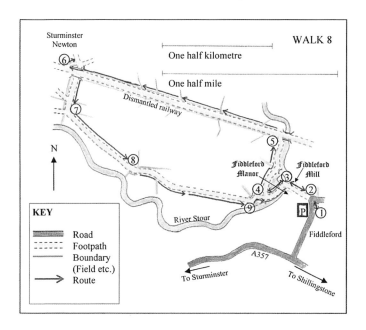

ROUTE

1. Leave the car park by the exit to the road and turn left (roughly north). Follow the road for 50 yards (45 metres) until it turns sharply right opposite a made-up drive on the left.

2. Turn left (roughly west) on to the drive (signposted for a footpath "Sturminster Newton 1 (1¾ via Railway Path)") and follow it for 100 yards (90 metres), until you reach an old water mill building on your right with a footbridge to its left.

3. Cross the bridge, turn left (roughly south-west), and follow the footpath across two bridges over the River Stour to a kissing gate on the far side.
Arrowhead and Fringed and Yellow Water-lilies can be seen in the water near the mill.

4. Go through the kissing gate and turn right (roughly north) on to a footpath (signposted "Sturminster Newton via railway path 1¼"). Follow the footpath beside the river, along the right edge of two fields linked by a small wooden bridge, for 400 yards (360 metres) until you reach a kissing gate near a rebuilt former railway bridge.
Arrowhead, Common Club-rush, Common Meadow-rue, Meadowsweet, Water Chickweed, Wild Teasel and Yellow Water-lily grow in or by the river.

5. Go through the kissing gate, turn left, and, after a few yards, turn half left (roughly west) on to a footpath along the line of the old railway. Continue on the footpath for just over ½ mile (1 km) until, soon after it crosses a bridge, it is joined by another footpath on your right.
    Great Willowherb, Hedgerow Crane's-bill, Hemlock, Meadowsweet, Tansy and Welted Thistle grow beside the footpath.

6. Turn sharply right on to this footpath, go down some steps and follow it round to the right underneath the bridge to a kissing gate. Go through the kissing gate and continue on the footpath (roughly south), along the right edge of two fields for 175 yards (160 metres), until you reach a kissing gate on the far side of the second field. There is an excellent view of the hill-fort on Hamblebon Hill to your left (roughly east) from the first field.

7. Go through the kissing gate into another field and turn half left (roughly south-east) on to a footpath (signposted "Fiddleford Manor Fiddleford Mill ¾"). Follow the footpath across the field for ¼ mile (400 metres) with the River Stour on your right until you reach a large metal gate and kissing gate on the far side.

Opposite: *View north along the River Stour from Fiddleford Mill.*
Below: *Fringed Water-lily*

Arrowhead

Named from the distinctive shape of its upper leaves, Arrowhead is found in slow-moving or still water close to Fiddleford Mill.

The plants have their roots in mud beneath the water and attractive spikes of flowers rising a foot (30 cm) or more above its surface. Arranged in whorls of three, the flowers are about ¾ inch (2 cm) across and have three snowy white petals, each with a purple patch at its base. The flowers at the bottom of each spike are female, while those above are male, their purplish stamen tips themselves shaped like arrowheads! Besides the upper leaves held above the water, there are others, oval in shape, floating on the surface, and, hidden from view, very long narrow ones beneath.

Rather uncommon in Dorset, this most appealing plant is found mainly along the River Stour and in other slow-moving water, especially around Wareham. It is fairly widespread in other parts of England.

"... large and long leaves, in shape ..... like a bearded broad arrowe heade: among which riseth up a fat and thicke stalk, ... having at the top many pretie white flowers, declining to a light carnation."

From *The Herbal or Generall Historie of Plantes*,
John Gerard

Above: *Arrowhead upper leaf*

Opposite: *Arrowhead flower head*

8. Go through the kissing gate into the next field, turn left and continue on the footpath (roughly east) for 650 yards (590 metres) along its left edge and then across a second field. Shortly before reaching the river, the footpath turns left (roughly north) across a small bridge over a stream (signposted "Fiddleford Mill Fiddleford Manor ¼").
Marsh Yellow-cress, Redshank and Tubular Water-dropwort grow beside the footpath in the second field, while Arrowhead is found in the stream under the small bridge.

9. Cross the bridge into a field and follow the footpath to your half right (roughly east) for nearly 50 yards (45 metres) until you reach the kissing gate you went through at the start of stage 4. Retrace your steps to the car park.

After your walk you may like to visit Fiddleford Manor to see its exceptionally fine wooden roofs. The Manor, which is in the care of English Heritage, can be reached directly from the car park: there is no entry charge.

Meadowsweet

You will see Meadowsweet's characteristic clusters of creamy white flowers frequently along the River Stour and the old railway line.

Rising above the surrounding vegetation, the plants grow up to about 5 feet (150 cm) tall. The fragrant flowers are about ¼ inch (6 mm) across with 4-6 spoon-shaped petals; each has many prominent stamens, giving the clusters a fuzzy look. The reddish-stalked leaves are silvery underneath and have about 2-4 pairs of large, toothed leaflets with small leaflets in between.

Although the name Meadowsweet may have originally arisen as the plant was used to flavour mead, it equally describes the pleasant smell it gives to its surroundings. It was also used as a painkiller as the sap contains chemicals similar to aspirin, which was named after Meadowsweet's old botanical name of *Spiraea ulmaria*.

Meadowsweet is common in Dorset near rivers and streams and in other wet places; it is widespread in Britain as a whole.

Opposite*: Foaming water at Fiddleford Mill.*

"While to mill by mill thou roamest,
And below the mill-weir foamest
   In the wildly-heaving pond.
And when, at night, the wheel may cease
To roll, may inmates sleep in peace."

From *The River Stour*,
William Barnes

Some of the flowers you may see on this walk

Agrimony *(Agrimonia eupatoria)*
Arrowhead *(Sagittaria sagittifolia)*
Black Medick *(Medicago lupulina)*
Black Mustard *(Brassica nigra)*
Borage *(Borago officinalis)*
Broad-leaved Willowherb *(Epilobium montanum)*
Bush Vetch *(Vicia sepium)*
Canadian Fleabane *(Conyza canadensis)*
Common Broomrape *(Orobanche minor)*
Common Club-rush *(Schoenoplectus lacustris)*
Common Mallow *(Malva sylvestris)*
Common Meadow-rue *(Thalictrum flavum)*
Common Poppy *(Papaver rhoeas)*
Common Toadflax *(Linaria vulgaris)*
Corn Marigold *(Chrysanthemum segetum)*
Dewberry *(Rubus caesius)*
Field Bindweed *(Convolvulus arvensis)*
Foxglove *(Digitalis purpurea)*

Fringed Water-lily *(Nymphoides peltata)*
Great Willowherb *(Epilobium hirsutum)*
Hedge Bedstraw *(Galium mollugo)*
Hedge Bindweed *(Calystegia sepium)*
Hedgerow Crane's-bill *(Geranium pyrenaicum)*
Hemlock *(Conium maculatum)*
Hemlock Water-dropwort *(Oenanthe crocata)*
Hemp-agrimony *(Eupatorium cannabinum)*
Herb-Robert *(Geranium robertianum)*
Hogweed *(Heracleum sphondylium)*
Indian Balsam, Himalayan Balsam *(Impatiens glandulifera)*
Knotgrass *(Polygonum aviculare)*
Lesser Burdock *(Arctium minus)*
Lesser Stitchwort *(Stellaria graminea)*
Marsh Ragwort *(Senecio aquaticus)*
Marsh Yellow-cress *(Rorippa palustris)*
Meadow Crane's-bill *(Geranium pratense)*
Meadowsweet *(Filipendula ulmaria)*

Meadow Vetchling *(Lathyrus pratensis)*
Mugwort *(Artemisia vulgaris)*
Musk-mallow *(Malva moschata)*
Nipplewort *(Lapsana communis)*
Oxeye Daisy *(Leucanthemum vulgare)*
Perennial Sow-thistle *(Sonchus arvensis)*
Perforate St. John's-wort *(Hypericum perforatum)*
Purple-loosestrife *(Lythrum salicaria)*
Redshank *(Persicaria maculosa)*
Red Valerian *(Centranthus ruber)*
Rough Chervil *(Chaerophyllum temulum)*
Scentless Mayweed *(Tripleurospermum inodorum)*
Selfheal *(Prunella vulgaris)*
Smooth Hawk's-beard *(Crepis capillaris)*
Spear-leaved Orache *(Atriplex prostrata)*

Tansy *(Tanacetum vulgare)*
Tubular Water-dropwort *(Oenanthe fistulosa)*
Tufted Vetch *(Vicia cracca)*
Upright Hedge-parsley *(Torilis japonica)*
Water Chickweed *(Myosoton aquaticum)*
Water Figwort *(Scrophularia auriculata)*
Water-plantain *(Alisma plantago-aquatica)*
Welted Thistle *(Carduus crispus)*
White Campion *(Silene latifolia)*
White Water-lily *(Nymphaea alba)*
Wild Angelica *(Angelica sylvestris)*
Wild Rose *(Rosa agg.)*
Wild Teasel *(Dipsacus fullonum)*
Winter-cress *(Barbarea vulgaris)*
Yellow Water-lily *(Nuphar lutea)*

Opposite left*: Water Chickweed*
Opposite right*: Great Willowherb*
Below left*: Wild Teasel*
Below right*: Welted Thistle*

WALK 9

HEATHLAND FLOWERS
IN LATE SUMMER
Stoborough Heath National Nature Reserve

A late summer walk over unspoilt heathland in Purbeck. We start by following the path of an old clay tramway, before joining a track over heathland rich in interesting flowers. We continue on the track over grassland before returning to the car park along minor roads.

Please keep strictly to the route - there are dangerous bogs on the heath.

Time of year:	mid-July to early September
Distance:	about 2½ miles (4 km)
Difficulty:	easy with no appreciable hills
Parking:	Stoborough Heath car park at SY 938 863 (free)
Directions to car park:	from Wareham take the A351 south towards Swanage. After 1½ miles (2½ km) turn left at a roundabout on to the B3075 (signposted "Stoborough"). After 400 yards (360 metres) turn right (signposted "Ridge 1 Arne 4"). After 750 yards (685 metres) turn right at a crossroads (signposted "Arne village and church 3") and continue for 650 yards (590 metres) until you reach the entrance to the car park on your right.
Ordnance Survey maps:	1:50,000 Landranger 195 Bournemouth & Purbeck 1:25,000 Explorer OL 15 Purbeck & South Dorset
Public transport:	40 bus between Poole and Swanage stops in Stoborough Green (check timetable)
Refreshments:	in Stoborough and Wareham
Toilets:	none

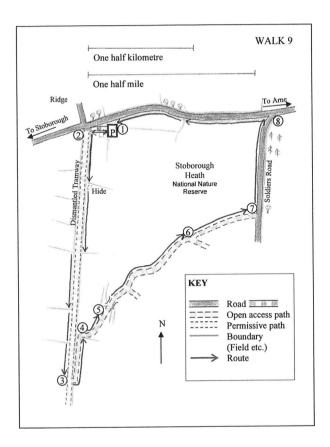

ROUTE

1.   Leave the car park by the gate where you entered and follow the footpath to the left of the entrance track (roughly west) for 100 yards (90 metres) until you reach an information board for Stoborough Heath National Nature Reserve with a waymark for a permissive path on your left.

2.   Turn left (south) on to the path which follows the route of an old clay tramway. Follow the path, going through a gate after 600 yards (550 metres) and a second gate after a further 500 yards (460 metres). Continue on the path until you reach a gate on your left, opposite a post waymarked with a blue arrow, 150 yards (135 metres) beyond the second gate. *Purple-loosestrife and Trailing St. John's-wort grow beside the path, while the reddish pink flowers of Dorset Heath can be seen in the wet heathland to your left.*

Bog Asphodel

This attractive member of the Lily family is found in the boggy parts of Stoborough Heath.

The plants are about 12 inches (30 cm) tall with spikes of bright yellow flowers shining like torches against the dull background. The flowers are star-shaped and about ½ inch (1¼ cm) across, with 6 narrow pointed petal-like parts surrounding 6 very hairy yellow stamens with orange tips. After flowering, the whole plant turns an attractive deep orange. A few small narrow, pointed leaves clasp the stem, while others, larger and iris-like, grow from the base.

The plant was formerly used as a yellow hair-dye. Its scientific name is *Narthecium ossifragum*: the second part comes from the Latin for bone-breaking as it was believed that eating the plants caused brittleness in sheep's bones, although it is actually due to the lack of nutrients in the poor soils where they grow.

In Dorset, Bog Asphodel is found mostly in the Poole Basin, where it is fairly common in bogs and on wet heaths; it is widespread in western and northern Britain.

Opposite: *A spike of Bog Asphodel, shining like a yellow torch.*
Below: *Bog Asphodel clump.*

3. Turn left (east) through the gate and almost immediately turn left again on to a grassy track, waymarked with a blue arrow on a post. Follow the track (north) - reversing your direction in stage 2 - until after 200 yards (180 metres) it turns right at a post waymarked with a blue arrow.
    Lesser Skullcap, Marsh Pennywort and the tiny Allseed grow along the track, while Dorset Heath is found in wet ground to your right. Bog Asphodel, Marsh St. John's-wort and the insectivorous Pale Butterwort and Sundews can be seen in the boggy area ahead of you. Bog-myrtle also grows around here and its distinctive smell permeates the heathland air.

4. Follow the track round to the right (east) and as it bears left (roughly north-east) after a few yards. Continue on the track for 120 yards (110 metres) until you reach a small wooden gate next to a large gate.

5. Go through the small gate, cross a bridge over a stream and continue on the track (generally north-east) for 650 yards (590 metres), until it forks just before a post on your right waymarked for permissive paths.
    Marsh Gentian can be seen in the wet area to your left from mid-August, while Dodder is found on drier ground beside the track.

6. Take the left hand fork (roughly north-east) - in the direction of a conifer plantation - and continue on the track over grassland (roughly north-east then east) for 450 yards (410 metres), passing under power lines halfway along, until you reach a road. There are good views from the track to your half left (roughly north) towards the River Frome.
   Common Centaury, Eyebright and Yellow Bartsia grow beside the track.
7. Turn left (roughly north) on to the road and continue for 500 yards (460 metres) until you reach a T- junction just after a cattle grid.
   Agrimony grows on the road verges while Blue Fleabane is found by a forest entrance gate on your right. You may also spot the tiny Chaffweed on the verge to your right shortly before the cattle grid.
8. Turn left (west) at the T-junction and continue on the road for just over ½ mile (nearly 1 km) until you reach the car park on your left.

Opposite above*: View north over Stoborough Heath towards the River Frome.*
Opposite below*: Allseed*
Right above*: Marsh St. John's-wort*
Right below*: Blue Fleabane*

Dodder

"Dodder on furze spreads ruddy shawl
Clasped by pink pearls."

From *Groundsel*,
Andrew Young

Dodder is a parasite on gorse and heather and can be found where they grow on the drier parts of Stoborough Heath.

The plants take root in soil, but quickly attach themselves to the stems of their host where they begin to feed from it. Once the plants are established, the roots die and a tangled web of long red thread-like stems twines round the host.

Pleasantly scented pale pink flowers are borne on the stems in dense rounded heads about ¼ inch (6 mm) across. Each bell-shaped flower is about ⅛ inch (3 mm) across with 5 pointed petal lobes and protruding stamens. There are no leaves; instead tiny scales grow on the stems.

Dodder is quite frequent in Dorset on heaths in the Poole Basin and the far west of the county; it is also sometimes found on chalky soils growing on members of the pea or other families. It has declined in Britain over the past 75 years due to the loss of lowland heathland to agriculture, building and forestry, and the ploughing of chalk downlands.

Opposite: A spike of Heather decorated with Dodder flowers.

Some of the flowers you may see on this walk

Agrimony *(Agrimonia eupatoria)*
Allseed *(Radiola linoides)*
Autumn Hawkbit *(Leontodon autumnalis)*
Bell Heather *(Erica cinerea)*
Bird's-foot *(Ornithopus perpusillus)*
Blue Fleabane *(Erigeron acer)*
Bog Asphodel *(Narthecium ossifragum)*
Bog Pimpernel *(Anagallis tenella)*
Buck's-horn Plantain *(Plantago coronopus)*
Cat's-ear *(Hypochaeris radicata)*
Chaffweed *(Anagallis minima)*
Common Bird's-foot-trefoil, Eggs-and-Bacon *(Lotus corniculatus)*
Common Centaury *(Centaurium erythraea)*
Common Fleabane *(Pulicaria dysenterica)*
Common Knapweed, Hardheads *(Centaurea nigra)*
Common Stork's-bill *(Erodium cicutarium)*
Common Vetch *(Vicia sativa)*
Creeping Cinquefoil *(Potentilla reptans)*
Creeping Thistle *(Cirsium arvense)*
Cross-leaved Heath *(Erica tetralix)*
Devil's-bit Scabious *(Succisa pratensis)*
Dodder *(Cuscuta epithymum)*
Dorset Heath *(Erica ciliaris)*
Dwarf Gorse *(Ulex minor)*
Dove's-foot Crane's-bill *(Geranium molle)*
Eyebright *(Euphrasia officinalis agg.)*
Fairy Flax *(Linum catharticum)*
Fen Bedstraw *(Galium uliginosum)*
Greater Bird's-foot-trefoil *(Lotus pedunculatus)*

Great Willowherb *(Epilobium hirsutum)*
Heather *(Calluna vulgaris)*
Heath Groundsel *(Senecio sylvaticus)*
Heath Milkwort *(Polygala serpyllifolia)*
Heath Speedwell *(Veronica officinalis)*
Hedge Bindweed *(Calystegia sepium)*
Hemp-agrimony *(Eupatorium cannabinum)*
Hop Trefoil *(Trifolium campestre)*
Lesser Centaury *(Centaurium pulchellum)*
Lesser Hawkbit (*Leontodon saxatilis)*
Lesser Spearwort *(Ranunculus flammula)*
Lesser Skullcap *(Scutellaria minor)*
Lousewort *(Pedicularis sylvatica)*
Marsh Gentian *(Gentiana pneumonanthe)*
Marsh Pennywort *(Hydrocotyle vulgaris)*
Marsh St. John's-wort *(Hypericum elodes)*
Marsh Thistle *(Cirsium palustre)*
Marsh Woundwort *(Stachys palustris)*
Meadow Buttercup *(Ranunculus acris)*
Meadowsweet *(Filipendula ulmaria)*
Mouse-ear-hawkweed *(Pilosella officinarum)*
Mugwort *(Artemisia vulgaris)*
Musk-mallow *(Malva moschata)*
Nipplewort *(Lapsana communis)*
Oxeye Daisy *(Leucanthemum vulgare)*
Pale Butterwort *(Pinguicula lusitanica)*
Perennial Sow-thistle *(Sonchus arvensis)*
Perforate St. John's-wort *(Hypericum perforatum)*
Purple-loosestrife *(Lythrum salicaria)*
Red Bartsia *(Odontites vernus)*

Redshank *(Persicaria maculosa)*
Round-leaved Sundew *(Drosera rotundifolia)*
Sand Spurrey *(Spergularia rubra)*
Scarlet Pimpernel *(Anagallis arvensis* ssp. *arvensis)*
Selfheal *(Prunella vulgaris)*
Sheep's Sorrel *(Rumex acetosella)*
Slender St. John's-wort (*Hypericum pulchrum)*
Smooth Hawk's-beard *(Crepis capillaris)*
Smooth Sow-thistle *(Sonchus oleraceus)*
Spear Thistle *(Cirsium vulgare)*

Square-stalked St. John's-wort *(Hypericum tetrapterum)*
Thyme-leaved Speedwell *(Veronica serpyllifolia)*
Tormentil *(Potentilla erecta)*
Trailing St. John's-wort *(Hypericum humifusum)*
Tufted Vetch *(Vicia cracca)*
Wild Angelica *(Angelica sylvestris)*
Wild Carrot *(Daucus carota* ssp. *carota)*
Wood Sage *(Teucrium scorodonia)*
Yarrow *(Achillea millefolium)*
Yellow Bartsia *(Parentucellia viscosa)*
Yellow-rattle *(Rhinanthus minor)*

Right*: The strikingly beautiful Marsh Gentian*

WALK 10

LATE SUMMER FLOWERS ON
AN ANCIENT COMMON
Corfe Common

A late summer walk near Corfe Castle in Purbeck. Starting in the town, we follow a footpath along the side of a field to the northern edge of Corfe Common. We cross the Common to its southernmost point, seeing a variety of attractive flowers of acid grassland and wet places. We then re-cross the Common by a different route, with excellent views of the castle and surrounding hills, before retracing our steps to the car park.

Time of year:	mid-July to early September
Distance:	about 2 miles (3 km)
Difficulty:	moderately easy, but with some uphill sections; often muddy in places
Parking:	car park at SY 959 818 (charge)
Directions to car park:	from Wareham take the A351 south towards Swanage. On reaching Corfe Castle town centre, turn right, immediately after the Greyhound public house on your right and just before a pedestrian crossing, into Market Square. Shortly afterwards, turn left into West Street and continue for 300 yards (275 metres) until you reach the entrance to the car park on your right.
Ordnance Survey maps:	1:50,000 Landranger 195 Bournemouth & Purbeck 1:25,000 Explorer OL 15 Purbeck & South Dorset
Public transport:	40 bus between Poole and Swanage stops in Corfe Castle (check timetable)
Refreshments:	in Corfe Castle
Toilets:	at car park

ROUTE

1. Leave the car park at the far right end from where you entered, through a kissing gate, waymarked for two National Trust footpaths, into a field. Take the footpath going along the left edge of the field and continue (roughly south-west) for 250 yards (230 metres) until you reach a waymarked kissing gate on the far side.

2. Go through the kissing gate and follow the footpath (roughly south-west) for 50 yards (45 metres) through a wooded area until you reach a gate waymarked for a bridleway running in two directions.

3. Go through the gate and turn left (south) on to the bridleway, which after 30 yards (27 metres) bears

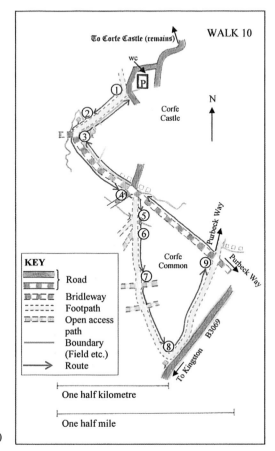

left (south-east) and emerges from trees on to Corfe Common. Continue on the bridleway for 400 yards (360 metres) until you reach a small waymarked metal gate. There are good views to your right (south) towards Kingston and behind you (north-west) to the Purbeck Hills.

Autumn Hawkbit, Betony, Chamomile, Common Knapweed, Harebell and Lesser Hawkbit are found along here.

4. Pass to the right of the gate and continue for a few yards until you reach a road with a cattle grid on your left. Cross the road and turn half right (roughly south) on to a National Trust footpath waymarked on a wooden post. Continue on the footpath (roughly south) downhill for 120 yards (110 metres) until you reach two small wooden bridges.

5. Cross the bridges, follow the footpath as it bears slightly left (roughly south), ignoring a footpath to the right, and continue uphill for 60 yards (55 metres) until you reach a marker post waymarked for two National Trust footpaths.

6. Take the footpath going straight ahead (roughly south) and continue uphill for 275 yards (250 metres) until you reach another marker post at the top. As you cross the Common there are superb views behind you (north) to the castle in the gap between the hills on either side.

    There is an attractive mixture of flowers here in August including Betony, Devil's-bit Scabious (with white, pink, blue or mauve flower heads), Goldenrod, Harebell, Saw-wort and Tormentil.

7. Continue straight ahead on the footpath (just east of south) downhill for 350 yards (320 metres) until you meet a crossing footpath, shortly after the footpath bears left (roughly east) through a boggy area and a few yards from a kissing gate at a road.

    As you go downhill Betony, Harebell and Saw-wort can be seen in good numbers, while Bog Pimpernel, Greater Bird's-foot-trefoil, Lesser Skullcap, Lesser Spearwort, Marsh Pennywort, Marsh Ragwort, Marsh St. John's-wort, Pale Butterwort and Square-stalked St. John's-wort grow in the boggy area and uphill to the left.

__Opposite__: Centuries of grazing have contributed to the richness of the flowers on Corfe Common.
__Right above__: Harebell
__Right below__: Slender St. John's-wort

Chamomile

"For though the camomile,
the more it is trodden on, the
faster it grows, yet youth, the
more it is wasted, the sooner
it wears."

From *Henry IV Part I*,
William Shakespeare

Popular for lawns in Elizabethan times, Chamomile is found in short grassland on Corfe Common. Here it benefits from grazing and trampling by livestock, which suppress competition from stronger growing plants.

The plants are kept low by constant grazing; their spreading stems, bearing the long-stalked flower heads, rise just a few inches above the ground. Each flower head is about 1 inch (2½ cm) across and like a large Daisy with a noticeably domed yellow centre.

The feathery leaves are deeply divided into tiny pointed segments and have a distinctive smell of apples when crushed - often quite noticeable as you walk over the plants when crossing the Common.

Chamomile is found in Dorset in moist, well-grazed acid grassland. It has declined dramatically in the county over the past 75 years, partly due to lack of grazing, and is now confined to a very small number of sites, including the cricket field at Pamphill. It has also declined in many other parts of Britain during the same period.

Opposite*: Zigzag Clover*

Saw-wort

Resembling a spineless thistle, Saw-wort is plentiful in the grassy areas of Corfe Common, often growing beside Betony (see painting opposite).

The plants are usually about 18 inches (45 cm) tall, slender and graceful, with flower heads held on branched, sparsely-leaved solid stems. The sweet-smelling flower heads are purple, up to about 1 inch (2½ cm) across and contain many tiny flowers, while beneath are neatly arranged purplish bracts. Male and female flowers are borne on separate plants.

The leaves are narrow and pointed and sometimes lobed; their fine saw-like teeth give the plant its name. They were formerly used to make a yellow-green dye for wool.

Saw-wort is fairly widespread in Dorset in old grassland and in wet places; as at Corfe Common, it can be found in great numbers where conditions are suitable. It is quite common in South West England and Wales.

8. Turn left (roughly north-east) on to the crossing footpath and follow it (roughly north-east then north), at first uphill then downhill, ignoring all side turnings and crossing paths, for 550 yards (500 metres) until you reach a National Trust marker stone - looking like a small triangulation pillar - close to where the footpath is crossed by a bridleway. As you descend there are attractive views ahead of you (roughly north) to the castle and the hills on either side.
Slender St. John's-wort is found beside the footpath.

9. Turn left (roughly north-west) just past the marker stone on to the bridleway and continue for 550 yards (500 metres), following a line towards a prominent track on a distant hill, until you reach the place where you crossed the road at stage 4. Retrace your steps to the car park.
Chamomile and Zigzag Clover can be seen along here.

Opposite: *Betony and Saw-wort are often found together on Corfe Common.*

Some of the flowers you may see on this walk

Autumn Hawkbit *(Leontodon autumnalis)*
Agrimony *(Agrimonia eupatoria)*
Bell Heather *(Erica cinerea)*
Betony *(Stachys officinalis)*
Bitter-vetch *(Lathyrus linifolius)*
Black Medick *(Medicago lupulina)*
Bog Pimpernel *(Anagallis tenella)*
Broad-leaved Willowherb *(Epilobium montanum)*
Chamomile *(Chamaemelum nobile)*
Cat's-ear *(Hypochaeris radicata)*
Common Bird's-foot-trefoil, Eggs-and-Bacon *(Lotus corniculatus)*
Common Centaury *(Centaurium erythraea)*
Common Fleabane *(Pulicaria dysenterica)*
Common Knapweed, Hardheads *(Centaurea nigra)*
Common Valerian *(Valeriana officinalis)*
Creeping Cinquefoil *(Potentilla reptans)*
Creeping Thistle *(Cirsium arvense)*
Cross-leaved Heath *(Erica tetralix)*
Devil's-bit Scabious *(Succisa pratensis)*
Dove's-foot Crane's-bill *(Geranium molle)*
Eyebright *(Euphrasia officinalis agg.)*
Field Bindweed *(Convolvulus arvensis)*
Fen Bedstraw *(Galium uliginosum)*
Germander Speedwell *(Veronica chamaedrys)*
Goldenrod *(Solidago virgaurea)*
Greater Bird's-foot-trefoil *(Lotus pedunculatus)*
Greater Plantain *(Plantago major)*
Great Willowherb *(Epilobium hirsutum)*

Hairy Buttercup *(Ranunculus sardous)*
Harebell *(Campanula rotundifolia)*
Heath Bedstraw *(Galium saxatile)*
Heath Milkwort *(Polygala serpyllifolia)*
Heath Speedwell *(Veronica officinalis)*
Heath Spotted-orchid *(Dactylorhiza maculata)*
Hedge Bindweed *(Calystegia sepium)*
Hedge Woundwort *(Stachys sylvatica)*
Herb-Robert *(Geranium robertianum)*
Hogweed *(Heracleum sphondylium)*
Lesser Hawkbit *(Leontodon saxatilis)*
Lesser Skullcap *(Scutellaria minor)*
Lesser Spearwort *(Ranunculus flammula)*
Lesser Trefoil *(Trifolium dubium)*
Lousewort *(Pedicularis sylvatica)*
Marsh Pennywort *(Hydrocotyle vulgaris)*
Marsh Ragwort *(Senecio aquaticus)*
Marsh St. John's-wort *(Hypericum elodes)*
Marsh Thistle *(Cirsium palustre)*
Marsh Willowherb *(Epilobium palustre)*
Meadow Buttercup *(Ranunculus acris)*
Meadowsweet *(Filipendula ulmaria)*
Meadow Vetchling *(Lathyrus pratensis)*
Mouse-ear-hawkweed *(Pilosella officinarum)*
Nipplewort *(Lapsana communis)*
Pale Butterwort *(Pinguicula lusitanica)*
Prickly Sow-thistle *(Sonchus asper)*
Ragged-Robin *(Lychnis flos-cuculi)*
Red Bartsia *(Odontites vernus)*
Red Campion *(Silene dioica)*
Red Clover *(Trifolium pratense)*
Redshank *(Persicaria maculosa)*
Saw-wort *(Serratula tinctoria)*

Selfheal *(Prunella vulgaris)*
Sheep's Sorrel *(Rumex acetosella)*
Silverweed *(Potentilla anserina)*
Slender St. John's-wort (*Hypericum pulchrum)*
Spear Thistle *(Cirsium vulgare)*
Square-stalked St. John's-wort *(Hypericum tetrapterum)*
Strawberry Clover *(Trifolium fragiferum)*
Tormentil *(Potentilla erecta)*
Tufted Vetch *(Vicia cracca)*
Upright Hedge-parsley *(Torilis japonica)*
Wall Speedwell *(Veronica arvensis)*
Wild Angelica *(Angelica sylvestris)*
Wood Sage *(Teucrium scorodonia)*
Yarrow *(Achillea millefolium)*
Zigzag Clover *(Trifolium medium)*

Right above: *Pale Butterwort - the plant supplements its nutrients with insects caught in the sticky leaves.*

Right below: *Lousewort*

A plain in front of me,
  And there's the road
Upon it. Wide country,
  And, too, the road!

Past the first ridge another,
  And still the road
Creeps on. Perhaps no other
  Ridge for the road?

Ah! Past that ridge a third,
  Which still the road
Has to climb furtherward -
  The thin white road!

Sky seems to end its track;
  But no. The road
Trails down the hill at the back.
  Ever the road!

The Weary Walker,
Thomas Hardy

Opposite: The coast path at Durdle Door

BIBLIOGRAPHY

ALLAN, B., WOODS, P. (1993) *Wild Orchids of Scotland.* HMSO. Reprinted (1993).

BLAMEY, M., FITTER, R., FITTER, A. (2003) *Wild Flowers of Britain & Ireland.* A. & C. Black Publishers Ltd.

BLAMEY, M., GREY-WILSON, C. (1989) *The Illustrated Flora of Britain and Northern Europe.* Hodder and Stoughton.

* BOWEN, H.J.M. (2000) *The Flora of Dorset.* Pisces Publications.
An essential reference work for students of the Dorset flora.

* CRAMB, P. & M. (2003) *Wild Flowers of the Dorset Coast Path.* P. & M. Cramb.
A beginners' identification guide to flowers seen along the coast path.

* CRAMB, P. & M. (2006) *Wild Flower Walks in Dorset.* P. & M. Cramb.

* DORSET WILDLIFE TRUST (1997) *The Natural History of Dorset.* The Dovecote Press Ltd.

DRAPER, J. (1986) *Dorset, The Complete Guide.* The Dovecote Press Ltd. Revised Ed. (1996).

* EDWARDS, B. (2008) *Wildlife of the Jurassic Coast.* Coastal Publishing.
An excellent guide to coastal habitats, their flowers and other wildlife.

* EDWARDS, B., PEARMAN, D.A. (2004) *Dorset Rare Plant Register.* Dorset Environmental Records Centre in conjunction with the Botanical Society of the British Isles.
A detailed inventory of Dorset's rare plants and their locations.

FOLEY, M., CLARKE, S. (2005) *Orchids of the British Isles.* Griffin Press Publishing Ltd.

* GOOD, R. D. (1948) *A Geographical Handbook of the Dorset Flora.* Dorset Natural History and Archaeological Society.

GRIGSON, G. (1955) *The Englishman's Flora.* J. M. Dent & Sons Ltd. Reprinted (1987).

HAWKINS, D. (1983) *Hardy's Wessex.* Macmillan London Ltd.

* HORSFALL, A. (1991) *Names of Wild Flowers in Dorset.* A. Horsfall.

* JENKINSON, M. N. (1991) *Wild Orchids of Dorset.* Orchid Sundries Ltd.

LEGG, R. (1990) *Literary Dorset.* Dorset Publishing Company.

MABEY, R. (1996) *Flora Britannica.* Sinclair-Stevenson.

* MANSEL-PLEYDELL, J. C. (1874) *The Flora of Dorsetshire.* Privately printed. 2nd Ed. (1895).

MARREN, P. (1999) *Britain's Rare Flowers.* T. & A. D. Poyser Ltd.

MASSINGHAM, H. J. (1936) *English Downland.* Batsford.

NEWMAN, J., PEVSNER, N. (1972) *The Buildings of England: Dorset.* Penguin Books. Reprinted (1999).

POWYS, Ll. (1935) *Dorset Essays.* Bodley Head. Enlarged selection first published by Redcliffe Press Ltd. (1983).

* PRATT, E. A. (2008) *The Wild Flowers of the Isle of Purbeck, Brownsea and Sandbanks.* Brambleby Books.
  An outstanding local flora of this special area for wild flowers.

PRESTON, C. D., PEARMAN, D. A., DINES, T. D., Eds. (2002) *New Atlas of the British & Irish Flora.* Oxford University Press.

PUTNAM, B. (1984) *Roman Dorset.* The Dovecote Press Ltd. Reprinted (1993).

READER'S DIGEST (1981) *Field Guide to the Wild Flowers of Britain.* The Reader's Digest Association Limited. Reprinted (1989).

RICH, T. C. G., JERMY, A. C. (1998) *Plant Crib 1998.* Botanical Society of the British Isles.

* ROBERTS, S. (1984) *The Wild Flowers of Dorset.* The Dovecote Press Ltd. Reprinted (1989).

ROYAL COMMISSION ON HISTORICAL MONUMENTS (ENGLAND) (1975) *An Inventory of Historical Monuments in the County of Dorset. Volume 5, East Dorset.* HMSO.

RSPB *Garston Wood Nature Reserve Trail Guide.* RSPB.

STACE, C. (1991) *New Flora of the British Isles.* Cambridge University Press. 2nd Ed. (1997).

STEWART, A., PEARMAN, D. A., PRESTON, C. D., Eds. (1994) *Scarce Plants in Britain.* JNCC.

TARR, R. (1989) *National Trail Guide 11, South West Coast Path, Exmouth to Poole.* Aurum Press Ltd. in association with the Countryside Commission and the Ordnance Survey. Revised Ed. (2002).

* TOMLINSON, N., Ed. (1997) *The Flowering Plants of Chesil Beach at Portland.* Chesil Bank and the Fleet Nature Reserve.

TREVES, F. (1906) *Highways and Byways in Dorset.* Macmillan and Co., Ltd. Reprinted (1920).

WIGGINTON, M. J., Ed. (1999) *British Red Data Books. 1 Vascular Plants.* Joint Nature Conservation Committee. 3rd Ed.

WILSON, P., KING, M. (2003) *Arable Plants - a field guide.* WILDGuides Ltd.

YOUNG, A. (1945) *A Prospect of Flowers.* Jonathan Cape. Reprinted (1946).

YOUNG, A. (1950) *A Retrospect of Flowers.* Jonathan Cape.

YOUNG, A. (1974) *Complete Poems.* Secker & Warburg.

* denotes a publication including Dorset's wild flowers.

ORGANISATIONS TO JOIN

DORSET

Dorset Flora Group
Dorset Environmental Records Centre, Library Headquarters, Colliton Park, Dorchester, Dorset DT1 1XJ. Telephone: 01305 225081
Field meetings, opportunities to volunteer. Beginners encouraged.

Dorset Natural History and Archaeological Society
Dorset County Museum, High West Street, Dorchester, Dorset DT1 1XA.
Telephone: 01305 262735
Talks, field meetings, opportunities to volunteer.

Dorset Wildlife Trust
Brooklands Farm, Forston, Dorchester, Dorset DT2 7AA.
Telephone: 01305 264620
Talks, field meetings, opportunities to volunteer.

NATIONAL

Botanical Society of the British Isles
Hon. General Secretary, c/o Department of Botany, The Natural History Museum, Cromwell Road, London SW7 5 BD. Telephone: 020 7942 5000
Field meetings, opportunities to volunteer.

Plantlife International
14 Rollestone Road, Salisbury, Wiltshire SP1 1DX.
Telephone: 01722 342730
Opportunities to volunteer.

The RSPB
The Lodge, Sandy, Bedfordshire SG19 2DL. Telephone: 01767 680551
Local activities, opportunities to volunteer.

The National Trust
Membership Department, P.O. Box 39, Warrington WA5 7WD.
Telephone: 0870 458 4000
Local activities, opportunities to volunteer.